INTENTIONAL
DISCIPLESHIP SERIES

ORIENTATION TO DISCIPLESHIP
CAMPAIGN WORKBOOK

DAVID STEEL

ISBN-13: 978-1468027556
ISBN-10: 1468027557

To Joleen, Jonathan, Daniel, and Matthew,
my favorite Christ followers

Contents

WEEK FOUR

The Dynamics of Discipleship: What *Enables* Us to Follow Jesus?...........71

WEEK FIVE

The Destiny of Discipleship: What *Happens* When We Follow Jesus?.....................89

Preface to the Intentional Discipleship Series

Go and make disciples . . .
teaching them to obey everything I have commanded you.
JESUS CHRIST

I do not know of a denomination or local church in existence that has
as its goal to teach its people to do everything Jesus said.
I'm not talking about a whim or a wish, but a plan.[1]
DALLAS WILLARD

Does Jesus really expect us to teach people to obey everything he has commanded?[2] *Everything*?

Teaching people to obey *some* of the things Jesus commanded is one thing. But teaching them to obey *everything* he commanded?[3] That's going to take some serious planning! And yet Dallas Willard, a well-known Christian author, says he hasn't found a single church with a *plan* for carrying out this Great Commission. Is Willard's observation off base here or are we missing something obvious?

Having been a pastor for almost two decades, I have met many faithful ministers and church leaders whose sincerity and devotion to Christ are beyond question. I believe the problem Willard has identified is not a lack of *sincerity*. It's a lack of *intentionality*.

Here's the haunting question: *How can we claim to take the Great Commission seriously if we have no plan for carrying it out?* It's a question that first began to keep me awake at night right after I accepted my first pastorate in 1993. As the new Associate Pastor of

---

[1]Dallas Willard, *The Great Omission: Reclaiming Jesus's Essential Teachings on Discipleship* (New York, NY: Harper One, 2006), 61. See also pages 72-73.

[2]Michael Wilkins asserts that, "The Great Commission, which concludes Jesus' earthly ministry, is intended for the church, and in it we find the culmination of his purposes in calling and training disciples." Michael J. Wilkins, *Following the Master: A Biblical Theology of Discipleship* (Grand Rapids, MI: Zondervan), 120.

[3]A similar command is issued to Joshua in the Old Testament, where God expects him to be careful to do *everything* written in God's Law (Joshua 1:8).

Discipleship, my job was to champion the Great Commission in our congregation. So, I began to think seriously and strategically about how to engage people in practical discipleship. I soon realized that we needed more than a biblically sound philosophy of ministry. We needed some substantial and systematic disciple-making resources if we were going to teach people to obey everything Jesus commanded. With all the Bible-believing churches and para-church ministries in existence, I figured there must already be plenty of tools like that out there.

I was wrong.

While there has been some encouraging progress recently in the way discipleship is being taught in published resources, I suspect that the reason it's so difficult to find a church with a plan to teach people to obey everything Christ commanded is that it's equally difficult to find any disciple-making resources designed to help churches do that. The work of George Barna, a well-known Christian researcher, seems to bear this out. He concludes that, "There is a tremendous need for a more intentional focus on the discipleship process and for definition to the desired outcomes of such a process."[4] On a more positive note, Barna says, "Given the proper motivation, it seems that most believers would be willing to commit to a more demanding regimen of spiritual development."[5]

The resources that comprise the Intentional Discipleship Series, such as the one you hold in your hand, are designed to help address this strategic need and nagging spiritual hunger among us. This material, which is intended to be discussed with other Christ followers in a supportive small group context, is designed for churches that want to be deliberate about fulfilling the Great Commission. While no curriculum is exhaustive, we hope that the Intentional Discipleship Series material will give churches a solid platform on which to build a comprehensive and systematic disciple-making ministry.

What Discipleship Is Not

But before we get into what discipleship *is*, let's identify what it is *not*. Jesus warned us of at least three forms of spiritual phoniness that fall short of true discipleship.

---

[4]George Barna, *Growing True Disciples* (Ventura, CA: Issachar Resources, 2000), 47.
[5]Ibid.

First of all, Jesus teaches us that *drama is not discipleship*. That is, *acting* spiritual isn't the same as *being* spiritual. Jesus says, "Be careful not to do your "acts of righteousness"[6] before men, to be seen by them. If you do, you will have no reward from your Father in heaven" (Matthew 6:1). Jesus is not impressed by our showy displays of spirituality.

Second, Jesus teaches us that *dogma is not discipleship*. He had some stern words for people who elevated their own religious traditions above the teachings of Scripture: "You nullify the word of God for the sake of your tradition. You hypocrites!" (Matthew 15:6-7).

Finally, Jesus teaches us that *duplicity is not discipleship* either. Knowing the Scriptures—even teaching them—without intending to practice what they teach is not discipleship. It's hypocrisy. (See Matthew 23:1-4.)

Discipleship is *not* about managing our image, defending our religious tradition, or talking a good talk. It's about opening our hearts to the transforming power of Christ. This is what it means to be his disciple.

Packing Our Gear

As we prepare for this journey together, let's familiarize ourselves with the equipment we'll be taking with us.

A Compass. Just as hikers use a compass to stay headed in the right direction, so disciples of Jesus use the Bible to keep their life headed toward the goal. Out here, your spiritual Compass is vital equipment. For each of these expeditions in discipleship, you'll be consulting that Compass, making course corrections as needed. If you don't have a Bible, you'll need to get one. A study Bible can be particularly helpful. There are several excellent translations out there, but the one quoted throughout the Intentional Discipleship Series is the New International Version® (NIV®).

Topographical Maps. We'll also be consulting some colorful spiritual maps of the region that have been handed down to us generation after generation. These time-tested traveling companions are the work of some of Christ's most famous followers, including Augustine, Thomas à Kempis, William Law, Andrew Murray, Charles Spurgeon, D. L. Moody, Oswald Chambers, C. S. Lewis, and dozens more. Our forerunners have left us a

---

[6]In this context, Jesus points to giving to the needy and praying as examples of such "acts of righteousness."

wealth of information for navigating the course. We'll make good use of their discoveries by quoting them along the way.

Health Food. Given the length of our journey, we'll need to develop some disciplined nutritional habits along the way. That means regular intake of the Word of God. The Bible says, "Like newborn babies, crave pure spiritual milk, so that by it you may grow up in your salvation" (1 Peter 2:2). In addition to regular times of Bible study, you'll want to take in the Scripture memory verses provided along the way. Like a spiritual energy drink, these are a great source of spiritual nutrition. So, drink up—we don't want anyone fainting on the trail!

Safety Rope. Sometimes the discipleship terrain can get a little steep and treacherous. For this reason, these expeditions are best taken with fellow pilgrims. When tied together with cords of loving fellowship, our fellow disciples can break our fall and pull us up if we should lose our footing. As Scripture says, "Two are better than one, because they have a good return for their work: if one falls down, his friend can help him up" (Ecclesiastes 4:9-10).

Personal Journey Log. These spiritual excursions are meant to be savored! That's why we encourage you to log what you're experiencing and learning along the way. Be sure to take time to pause and record your reflections. It will greatly enhance the joy of the journey!

What to Expect

So here's what you can expect from this material:

1. *It's biblical.* These lessons are rooted not in the wisdom of men but in the Word of God, beginning with the teachings of Jesus himself.
2. *It's accessible.* Discipleship is not just for highly educated or disciplined people. These straightforward, easy-to-digest lessons are designed to make discipleship doable for *all* of us, from youth on up.
3. *It's inspirational.* Our companions and mentors on this journey are some of history's most inspirational Christ followers. Their writings express the profound truths of our faith in ways that stir us deeply and move us to action. You'll want to linger on their words.

4. *It's holistic.* Biblical discipleship is essentially three-dimensional, engaging our convictions,[7] our character,[8] and our conduct.[9]

5. *It's practical.* You won't be pumped full of heady doctrines, but you will be challenged to apply what you're learning to how you live each day.

6. *It's memorable.* To increase the likelihood of remembering what we're learning, we've included Scripture memory passages to help us internalize and revisit these truths throughout the day.

7. *It's sustainable.* Discipleship is not a program we "graduate" from. These materials are designed to foster spiritual habits for a *lifetime* of discipleship to Jesus.

8. *It's expandable and adaptable.* Not every group that engages this material will have the same questions and interests. But chances are that something you read or discuss together will strike a chord within your group and you'll want to explore that topic further. That's why we've included numerous footnotes in the lessons that can help facilitate further study on particular points of interest.

A Final Word

Finally, a word about discipleship programs in general. Fundamentally, discipleship is a *process*, not a *program*. Programs are simply a means to an end—not the end in themselves. But while it's true that discipleship is always *more* than a program, it's also true that discipleship is seldom *less* than a program. That is, effective discipleship typically requires some forethought and organization. That's where the right programs and curricula can be so helpful.

So, my prayer is that your congregation would become part of a swelling tide of churches that are intent on teaching their people to obey everything Jesus commanded, and that these Intentional Discipleship Series resources would play a strategic role in bringing that vision to reality.

---

[7]Romans 12:2, for example, tells us to "be transformed by the renewing of your mind."

[8]By *character* we mean our inner life, who we really are. People are often concerned with outward appearances, but God is interested in our hearts (1 Samuel 16:7).

[9]While we should never settle for a spirituality that's only concerned with outward conformity, we shouldn't *minimize* the importance of our conduct either (see, for example, Matthew 5:16, Philippians 1:27, and James 2:26).

May you and your church "grow in the grace and knowledge of our Lord and Savior Jesus Christ. To him be glory both now and forever! Amen" (2 Peter 3:18).

The Epic Expedition

ex·pe·di·tion [ek-spi-**dish**-*uh*n] (noun) an excursion, journey, or voyage made for some specific purpose

ep·ic [**ep**-ik] (adjective) impressive by virtue of greatness of size, scope, or heroism

Ever heard the story of the greatest expedition ever undertaken? No, it's not William Edward Parry's harrowing voyage to the North Pole in 1827. Nor is it Edmund Hillary's costly ascent of Mount Everest in 1953. It's not even the 1969 lunar landing of Apollo 11. One expedition eclipses all of these.

It happened two thousand years ago when the Greatest of Beings travelled the greatest of distances to fulfill the greatest of missions. God himself made the cosmic trek from heaven to earth to rescue those he loved. No playwright has ever dreamed up a story as epic as this one.

The hero is Jesus Christ, God's Son. Those he loves are lost and in grave danger. They've wandered into a spiritual wilderness so dark and so treacherous that it has become impossible for them to ever find their way out. Tragically, it's a wilderness of their own making. The darkness that engulfs them is the result of their rejection of God. Still, Jesus loves them. And he knows that unless he rescues them, they will perish.

So, Jesus launches a one-man search and rescue operation. Though his search takes him down, down, down into the depths of darkness, he will not be deterred. For him, this is not just about *rescue*. It's about *reunion*.

Ultimately, this epic expedition will cost the Son of God his life, making it the most expensive search and rescue ever undertaken. In what becomes the most stunning display of sacrificial love the world has ever known, the King of Glory willingly lays down his life to save those he loves. "Greater love has no one than this," he says, "that he lay down his life for his friends" (John 15:13). He then lay down on a cross, allowing himself to be nailed to this instrument of death. There he gave his life, that those he loves might live.

But that's not the end of the story. Three days later this divine hero rises triumphantly from the grave! Who can doubt the invincible power and matchless love of this champion!

What makes this story so compelling is not just that it actually happened (it did). What makes this story so unforgettable is that it's *our* story. *We* are the ones the Son of God came to save. *We* are the ones for whom he died! *We* are the ones he wants to reconcile to himself! *We are the ones!*

Jesus came to call us out of hiding. To forgive us. To heal us. To restore us. It's a call to humble repentance and faith. It's a call to trust Jesus as our Savior and Master, that we might experience new life now and into eternity. In fact, this Epic Expedition of his will not be complete until our journey is joined to his—until we spend every day with him, learning from him, delighting in him, being transformed by him.

This is one expedition you don't want to miss!

And can it be that I should gain
 An interest in the Savior's blood?
Died He for me, who caused His pain—
 For me, who Him to death pursued?
Amazing love! How can it be,
 That Thou, my God, shouldst die for me?

Long my imprisoned spirit lay,
 Fast bound in sin and nature's night;
Thine eye diffused a quickening ray—
 I woke, the dungeon flamed with light;
My chains fell off, my heart was free,
 I rose, went forth, and followed Thee.
—CHARLES WESLEY

Want to read about it for yourself? Grab a Bible and look up these passages:

John 3:16 | John 5:24 | John 10:10 | John 14:6 | Romans 3:23 | Romans 5:8 | Romans 6:23
Romans 10:9, 13 | 1 Corinthians 15:1-8 | Ephesians 2:8-9 | 1 Timothy 2:5 | Titus 3:5 | 1 Peter 3:18

Roll Call

We are born homesick—longing for a land and a way of life we have never
directly experienced, but which we know is somewhere,
or at least ought to exist.[1]
JAMES WILHOIT

Blessed are those whose strength is in you,
who have set their hearts on pilgrimage.
THE SONS OF KORAH, PSALM 84:5

Picture this. Your spiritual journey has brought you to a clearing at the base of a majestic mountain that towers over the surrounding foothills. You're scheduled to meet several other hikers here for a guided expedition to the summit, beginning with an extensive orientation at base camp in the foothills. Realizing you're early, you climb on top of a huge boulder to sit and reflect. From here you can see for miles. Peering down, your eyes trace the path your feet have trod—sometimes lumbering over rocky terrain and other times strolling through green pastures and fragrant meadows. Your gaze lingers at the fork in the road where you chose the narrow path that has brought you here. Having surveyed the distance you've already come, you spin slowly around, your eyes following the mountain trail as it winds its way upward and out of sight. Your heart leaps, as you anticipate the adventure that awaits you.

The other hikers are arriving now. Soon the intermittent sound of chirping birds and rustling squirrels gives way to the buzz of spirited conversation. The team leader interrupts with an announcement: "It's orientation time everybody! Let's gather 'round!"

Roll call is the first order of business. Your enthusiasm mounts as you hear the names of the others who have shown up for this expedition with you. But the best part is when

---

[1]James C. Wilhoit, *Spiritual Formation as if the Church Mattered: Growing in Christ through Community*, (Grand Rapids, MI: Baker Academic, 2008), 64.

you hear your own name called. You call out "Here!" with the kind of gusto that makes you think you're even more excited to be here than you realized.

With everyone present and accounted for, the leader lays down his clipboard and eyes the group like a wise and loving father who has something important to say to his children.

"It's one thing to *decide* to follow Jesus," he says. "But what does it mean to follow through on that decision day by day? What does it mean to be a disciple of Jesus? That's the question we need to address before we set out on this journey.

"Truth is, discipleship is not an extracurricular activity reserved only for 'hard core believers.'[2] Since the earliest days of the church, discipleship has been the call of *every* true believer in Jesus.[3] James Montgomery Boice was right:

> Discipleship is not a supposed second step in Christianity, as if one first becomes a believer in Jesus and then, if he chooses, a disciple. From the beginning, discipleship is involved in what it means to be a Christian.[4]

In other words, to come to Christ for salvation is to become his follower. To become his follower is to come to him for salvation. The two cannot be separated. Discipleship, then, is a matter of *necessity*.

"But discipleship is also a matter of *intentionality*. We don't make progress on this journey by accident. Nor do we somehow "drift" into spiritual maturity. If we could, then Jesus' many exhortations about how we should live would be unnecessary.

"Finally, discipleship is a matter of *urgency*. When Jesus calls us to follow him, he means right now.[5] David Brainerd was an eighteenth century missionary who understood

---

[2]Unfortunately, some popular devotional writers have contributed to this misconception. Oswald Chambers, for example, writes, "There is a difference between salvation and discipleship. A man can be saved by God's grace without becoming a disciple of Jesus Christ." Oswald Chambers, *Studies in the Sermon on the Mount* (Fort Washington, PA: Christian Literature Crusade, 1960), 93.

[3]As Wilkins points out, "By the time of the early church, as recorded in Acts, the term *disciple* was synonymous with the true believer in Jesus." Michael J. Wilkins, *Following the Master*, 37.

[4]James Montgomery Boice, *Christ's Call to Discipleship* (Grand Rapids, MI: Kregel, 1986), 16.

[5]See, for example, Luke 9:62.

this. He prayed: 'Oh, that I might not loiter in my heavenly journey.'[6] That's not a bad prayer for us as we begin this orientation to discipleship.

"So here's what we're going to do. We're going to spend the next five weeks exploring what it means to be a disciple of Jesus. Each day we're going to spend at least seven minutes alone with Jesus working through a daily meditation. Then, once each week, we're going to come together to discuss what he's teaching us. Our goal is to stay connected with Jesus (daily) and our fellow disciples (weekly) over a long enough time to form some habits that will prepare us for a lifetime of fruitful discipleship to Jesus.

"Each week we'll deal with a different question. Here's the agenda:

- Week 1: Why do we *want* to follow Jesus?
- Week 2: What does it *take* to follow Jesus?
- Week 3: How does following Jesus *work*?
- Week 4: What *enables* us to follow Jesus?
- Week 5: Where are we *headed* by following Jesus?

"Are you ready then?

"Let's get started by getting better acquainted. Here are some questions to help us do that."

Getting Acquainted

1. What comes to mind when you hear the word "discipleship"?

2. What experiences or resources have shaped your understanding of discipleship up to this point?

---

[6]Jonathan Edwards, ed., *The Life and Diary of David Brainerd* (Grand Rapids, MI: Baker, 2001), 104.

3. How important do you think discipleship is to the local church? Why?

4. How do you suppose our church might benefit from focusing on discipleship together for five weeks?

5. What about this orientation to discipleship are you looking forward to? What do you hope to get out of it?

6. Do you have any reservations or questions about what we're setting out to do?

The Desire for Discipleship:
Why Do We *Want* to Follow Jesus?

Turning around, Jesus saw them following and asked,
"What do you want?"
JOHN 1:38

Thou hast formed us for Thyself, and our hearts are restless
till they find rest in Thee.
ST. AUGUSTINE

It began as an ordinary day. Sea gulls cawed overhead. Gentle waves lapped at the sides of small fishing boats. The air was filled with the smell of fish and the voices of sun-baked fishermen preparing to shove off. Another routine day for a couple of first century Galilean fishermen.

But life-as-usual was about to be interrupted . . . *permanently.*

"Simon! Andrew!"

The brothers looked up from their nets to see who was calling. They recognized him as Jesus of Nazareth.

"Come, follow me," he said, "and I will make you fishers of men!"

Jesus may have been hated by the stodgy religious leaders, but for Simon and Andrew just being in Jesus' presence—hearing him teach and watching how he lived— stirred something deep in their souls.[1]

Come, follow me, and I will make you fishers of men.

---

[1]This is not their first encounter with Jesus. See John 1:35-42.

His invitation was still ringing in their ears as they looked at each other. They knew immediately what they would do. They dropped their nets and followed, becoming Jesus' first disciples (Matthew 4:18-20).

A short time later, Jesus appealed to another young man to follow him. This guy had a great-looking resume. He was a wealthy leader in the community and a model of Jewish piety. What rabbi wouldn't want this guy as his disciple! And yet this man was not happy. His bank account was full, but his soul was empty. He knew something was missing. So he decided to try Jesus.

"Good Teacher," the man asked Jesus, "What do I need to do to inherit eternal life."

Jesus discerned that the man had a toxic attachment to wealth, so he suggested that the man sell his stuff, give to the poor, and then come follow him. At this, the man walked away sad because he was unwilling to part with his wealth (Luke 18:18-25). Apparently, he wanted dollars more than he wanted discipleship.

What makes some people want to follow Jesus while others just walk away? And what makes some who *seem* to want to follow Jesus give up after awhile?[2]

More importantly, why do *you* want to follow Jesus? Your answer will determine the vitality and longevity of your discipleship to him. That's why we're going to spend this week looking into some biblical reasons for following Jesus in the hopes that he will purify and intensify our desire to follow him.

---

[2]For example, some people who followed Jesus for the free food (John 6:22-27) eventually gave up on following him altogether (John 6:66).

Day 1
We Have Found the Messiah

We have found the Messiah.
THE APOSTLE ANDREW

Perhaps the most important question a Christ follower must answer is the one Jesus asked his disciples in Matthew 16:15: "Who do you say I am?" Many people answer Jesus' question with something like, "You're a great spiritual teacher" or "You're a prophet." These same people may consider themselves to be disciples of Jesus, but Jesus doesn't—not if that's *all* they believe about him.[1]

Peter, on the other hand, answered Jesus' question with a timeless proclamation that reverberates in the heart of every true disciple of Jesus. He declared: "You are the Christ, the Son of the living God" (Matthew 16:16).

What was Peter saying here? The word *Christ* literally means "anointed one." It was a reference to the centuries-old expectation of a coming Messiah, a Savior who would redeem God's people. The writings of the Old Testament prophets all pointed to this Messiah, as Jesus himself explained to two of his disciples on the road to Emmaus after his resurrection (Luke 24:27). From the very beginning, God's plan, as revealed in Scripture, has centered on this Savior who would bring redemption to his people. Peter acknowledged Jesus as that long-awaited Savior.

Apparently, Peter was not the first to recognize Jesus as the Savior of the world. In fact, Peter's brother Andrew (the one who introduced Peter to Jesus) told Peter, "We have found the Messiah" (John 1:41). The next day Philip (another one of Jesus' original followers) told Nathanael, "We have found the one Moses wrote about in the Law, and about whom the prophets also wrote—Jesus of Nazareth, the son of Joseph" (John 1:45). Nathanael came to see Jesus for himself and during that encounter declared, "Rabbi, you are the Son of God; you are the King of Israel" (John 1:49).

---

[1]See, for example, Luke 18:18-22.

And as Christ's kingdom plan unfolded, it became abundantly clear that he was not just a Savior to the Jewish people but to the whole world![2] Even "doubting Thomas," when he touched Jesus' nail wounds after his resurrection, declared him to be "My Lord and my God!" (John 20.28).

Of course Jesus himself confirmed his identity as the Messiah on more than one occasion.[3]

We could say much more about who Jesus is (and we will!), but what every true disciple of Jesus recognizes is that he is the long-awaited Savior, whose sacrifice frees us from our sin.[4] And so we join those earliest disciples in proclaiming, "We have found the Messiah!" It's why we follow him.

Reflect

1. In your opinion, is Jesus still worth following if he's *not* the Messiah? Why or why not?

2. Who do *you* say Jesus is? Express this to him in prayer.

Remember (our Scripture memory passage of the week)
Jesus answered, "I am the way and the truth and the life. No one comes to the Father except through me" (John 14:6).

---

[2]See, for example, Matthew 24:14, Acts 9:15, Acts 10:45, and Romans 1:16.

[3]See, for example, John 4:25-26 and Matthew 26:63-64.

[4]This, of course, is what we commemorate each time we partake of the Lord's Supper (Communion).

Day 2
God Draws Us

No one can come to me unless
the Father who sent me draws him.
JESUS CHRIST

Why do some people follow Jesus while others do not? Some point to upbringing or peer influence.[1] Others might explain it in terms of a person's predisposition toward either faith or reason. Others hold (whether spoken or unspoken) that it really comes down to one's intelligence—or lack thereof.

But what does *Jesus* have to say about this? According to Jesus, the reason a person chooses to follow him is that God the Father has drawn that person to himself.[2] So if you've come to Christ for salvation, you can rest assured that it's because God has drawn you to himself. What thrilling assurance this is! And what a powerful motivation it is as well! C. S. Lewis captures the significance of this truth when he urges us to, "Continue seeking Him with seriousness. Unless he wanted you, you would not be wanting Him."

So what does Jesus mean when he says that the Father *draws* us? He *doesn't* mean that God coerces us against our will. No, the Father opens our hearts to the truth about Jesus in such a way that we desire to follow him by our own will. Still, the Father can be very convincing, as Jesus points out a few verses earlier where he declares that, "All that the Father gives me will come to me" (John 6:37).

But it's not just the Father who draws us. The Son draws us too. Jesus said, "But I, when I am lifted up from the earth, will draw all men to myself" (John 12:32). He meant that by his crucifixion he would draw to himself all kinds of people—both Jews and Gentiles. And indeed he has!

---

[1]However, this seems to be contradicted by the fact that Jesus' own brothers did not believe in him during his earthly ministry (John 7:5).

[2]What a powerful antidote to spiritual pride this is! Coming to Christ is without a doubt the best decision we could ever make, but we can't take any of the credit for it.

Charles Spurgeon was right:

Jesus knows how by irresistible arguments addressed to the understanding, by mighty reasons appealing to the affections, and by the mysterious influence of His Holy Spirit operating upon all the powers and passions of the soul, so to subdue the whole man, that whereas he was once rebellious, he yields cheerfully to His government, subdued by sovereign love.[3]

Whenever I pause to consider how God has drawn me to himself—and that I would not even know him if he had not done so—I find myself wanting to pursue him all the more. As A. W. Tozer has said: "The impulse to pursue God originates with God, but the outworking of that impulse is our following hard after Him; and all the time we are pursuing Him we are already in His hand."[4]

Reflect
1. What do the biblical passages in today's reading reveal about the character of God?

2. How does your soul respond to the truth that God has drawn you to himself?

Remember (our Scripture memory passage of the week)
Jesus answered, "I am the way and the truth and the life. No one comes to the Father except through me" (John 14:6).

---

[3]Charles Spurgeon, *Morning and Evening Daily Readings* (Lynchburg, VA: The Old-Time Gospel Hour, n. d.), 423.
[4]A. W. Tozer, *The Best of A. W. Tozer: 52 Favorite Chapters*, compiled by Warren W. Wiersbe (Camp Hill, PA: Christian Publications, 1993), 13.

Day 3
Amazed by Jesus

People were overwhelmed with amazement.
"He has done everything well," they said.
MARK 7:37

You've probably heard the expression, "he walks on water." You may have even used it yourself. It's a way of saying that someone is truly amazing, that he can do wonders. Do you know where that expression comes from? It comes from the biblical account of Jesus walking on the Sea of Galilee (Mark 6:47-52). The disciples who saw this were "completely amazed." No kidding!

So, if you know Jesus, then you know someone who can walk on water. Literally.

During his earthly ministry, Jesus amazed a lot of people. He didn't just walk on water (as if that weren't enough). He also set a man free from demon possession. People were amazed (Mark 5:1-20). When Jesus healed a deaf and mute man people were "overwhelmed with amazement" (Mark 7:31-37). And when Jesus healed a paralytic, people were "amazed" and "filled with awe" (Luke 5:17-26). Others were "completely astonished" when he raised a young girl from the dead (Mark 5:21-43). The Bible records dozens of other miracles that Jesus performed. But that's not the half of it. "Jesus did many other things as well. If every one of them were written down, I suppose that even the whole world would not have room for the books that would be written" (John 21:25).

But it wasn't just the miracles that Jesus performed that amazed people. They were also amazed, for example, at the authority of his teaching (Mark 1:22). In fact, the temple guards sent by the chief priests and Pharisees to arrest Jesus couldn't bring themselves to do it because, as they reported, "No one ever spoke the way this man does" (John 7:46).

The crowds were amazed at his zeal when it came to the Heavenly Father's values (Mark 11:18). Pilate was amazed at his meekness (Mark 15:1-5). And his critics were astonished by his invincible wisdom (Luke 20:20-26).

Jesus is amazing. So, the next time someone asks you why you follow Jesus, tell them it's because he walks on water . . . and a whole lot more!

Reflect

1. What is it about Jesus that amazes you?

2. Given all the amazing things Jesus can do, what would you like him to do for you personally? Tell him in prayer.

Remember (our Scripture memory passage of the week)

Jesus answered, "I am the way and the truth and the life. No one comes to the Father except through me" (John 14:6).

Day 4
Rest for Our Souls

Come to me, all you who are weary and burdened, and I will give you rest.
Take my yoke upon you and learn from me, for I am gentle and humble in heart,
and you will find rest for your souls.
For my yoke is easy and my burden is light.
JESUS CHRIST

To those who are weighed down and worn out by the oppressive demands and disappointments of life, Jesus offers this freeing invitation: *Come to me. I will give you the rest you need—the kind of rest that washes over and rejuvenates your soul.*

Notice that the invitation is for *all* who are weary and burdened. Surely, that includes you and me. *That's* good news!

Notice also how we obtain this kind of inner rest and freedom: by taking on Jesus' yoke and learning from him. What does Jesus mean by this?

A yoke is a wooden bar that fits over the necks of animals, enabling them to pull a heavy load. Not surprisingly, Scripture often uses "yoke" as a metaphor for servitude. But here Jesus uses the term as a metaphor for the discipline we know as discipleship.[1]

What is surprising is Jesus' paradoxical way of referring to his "easy yoke" and his "light burden." Here's one yoke that's *not* oppressive. Here's one burden that's *not* heavy. Whatever demands discipleship may place on us (and we'll talk about these demands next week), they're actually easy and light—especially when compared to the demands of life *without* Christ. That's because when we take on *his* yoke, when we submit ourselves to him and learn from him, we enter into an intimate mentorship with the one person uniquely qualified to teach us the will and ways of God (see Matthew 11:27).

In Jesus' immediate audience there were plenty of people who were wearied and burdened by their own sense of spiritual failure. Their discouragement was due in part to

---

[1]D. A. Carson, *Matthew*, vol. 8 in *The Expositor's Bible Commentary*, ed. Frank E. Gaebelein (Grand Rapids, MI: Zondervan, 1984), 278.

the teachers of the law and the Pharisees who were tying up heavy loads and putting them on people's shoulders without so much as lifting a finger to help (see Matthew 23:4). To these downcast individuals Jesus says in effect, "You're wearing the wrong yoke. Try mine. Unlike the oppressive yoke of guilt you've been under, my yoke is light because I bear it with you. I'm a gentle teacher. I will strengthen and equip you, not crush you."

If we truly understand our discipleship to Jesus for what it is—learning and liberation for our souls—then it won't be a burden. On the contrary, this yoke carries with it the prospect of a truly satisfied soul.

Thomas à Kempis, a fifteenth century disciple, expressed the wonder of it all when he prayed,

> Angels and archangels stand in awe of thee—holy and righteous men do fear thee— and sayest thou, "Come ye all unto me?" Unless thou, O Lord, didst say this, who would believe it to be true? And unless thou didst command it, who could attempt to draw near?[2]

Reflect

1. When does your soul typically feel most "weary and burdened"?

2. What would it look like for you to take on Jesus' yoke and learn from him today?

Remember (our Scripture memory passage of the week)
Jesus answered, "I am the way and the truth and the life. No one comes to the Father except through me" (John 14:6).

---

[2]Thomas à Kempis, *The Imitation of Christ* (Chicago: M. A. Donohue & Co., 1900), Book 4, Chapter I, 3.

Day 5
Where Else Would We Go?

> *Lord, to whom shall we go?*
> *You have the words of eternal life.*
> THE APOSTLE PETER

At one point in Jesus' ministry when many of his fair-weather followers were turning back and no longer following him, Jesus asked his closest disciples, "You do not want to leave too, do you?" (John 6:67). That's when Peter came up with this profound reply: "Lord, to whom shall we go? You have the words of eternal life. We believe and know that you are the Holy One of God" (verses 68-69).

This is the basis of a disciple's persistence. Even when we're confounded and confused by some of Christ's teachings, we stay because of what we *do* understand — namely, that Jesus alone holds the keys to eternal life. When you've just seen Jesus walk on water as Peter had (see John 6:16-21), it seems a little silly to keep your options open in case a more authoritative teacher comes along.

We will always have unanswered questions. But there comes a time when we know enough about Jesus to be convinced that he's our only hope of ever sorting it all out. And that's why we persist in following him, even when others fall away. We simply have nowhere else to go.

Peter would later testify publicly that, "Salvation is found in no one else, for there is no other name under heaven given to men by which we must be saved" (Acts 4:12).

And Paul would declare that "There is one God and one mediator between God and men, the man Christ Jesus, who gave himself as a ransom for all men" (1 Timothy 2:5-6).

Where did Peter and Paul get such an idea? They got it from Jesus himself, who made it quite clear when he declared, "I am the way and the truth and the life. No one comes to the Father except through me" (John 14:6).

Whatever we still need to learn about Jesus, we know this much: he alone holds the keys to eternal life. And that's the reason we want to follow him. It's the reason we will continue following him over the long haul.

Reflect

1. When you experience doubts about your faith, what keeps you from walking away?

2. How does your soul respond to the truth that Jesus is the only way of salvation? Tell him in prayer.

Remember (our Scripture memory passage of the week)
Jesus answered, "I am the way and the truth and the life. No one comes to the Father except through me" (John 14:6).

Day 6
That We May Know God

This is eternal life: that they may know you, the only true God,
and Jesus Christ, whom you have sent.
JESUS CHRIST

Discipleship was not invented by Jesus. Various secular and religious forms of discipleship were already well established when Jesus called his first disciples.[1] And yet Jesus' brand of discipleship was different in one very important respect. With other forms of discipleship, the disciple would attach himself to the master in order to be associated with some transcendent cause or to learn a certain lifestyle to which the disciple aspired. The master, in that case, was a means to a greater end—namely, the mastery of some better way of life.

Not so with Jesus. When he calls us to follow him, he's not merely calling us to learn from him a better way of life, though he certainly will teach us that! The ultimate goal of discipleship to Jesus is to know the Master himself—not just to know what he knows, but to know *him*. Jesus is not the means to an end. He is the end.

Oswald Chambers put it this way:

There is a difference between devotion to principles and devotion to a person. Jesus Christ never proclaimed a cause; He proclaimed personal devotion to Himself. . . . Discipleship is based not on devotion to abstract ideals, but on devotion to a Person, the Lord Jesus Christ.[2]

---

[1] For a thorough discussion of this topic, see chapter five in Michael J. Wilkins, *Following the Master*.

[2] Oswald Chambers, *Studies in the Sermon on the Mount* (Fort Washington, PA: Christian Literature Crusade, 1960), 16-17.

"But wait a minute," someone will say. "Didn't Jesus come proclaiming the way of eternal life? Didn't he say that 'whoever believes in him should not perish but have eternal life' (John 3:16)? Wasn't this his *cause*?"

Indeed it was. But what is eternal life? Jesus answered that when he prayed, "This is eternal life: that they may know you, the only true God, and Jesus Christ, whom you have sent" (John 17:3). Jesus' "cause," then, is to make disciples who truly know him. No amount of knowledge *about* him or service *to* him can compare to the sheer joy of being *with* him. This is why we follow him.

The apostle Paul put it this way, "I consider everything a loss compared to the surpassing greatness of knowing Christ Jesus my Lord" (Philippians 3:8).

These words always stir something deep in my soul. On my best days, knowing Christ is the unrivaled passion of my life. I pray for more of those days. For all of us.

Reflect

1. How do you know if you're devoted to Christ himself or to "the Christian cause" in general? How does your desire to know him personally manifest itself in your life?

2. Do you need to be more intentional about getting to know Christ better? Ask him to show you if this is the case and what he would have you do about it.

Remember (our Scripture memory passage of the week)
Jesus answered, "I am the way and the truth and the life. No one comes to the Father except through me" (John 14:6).

Day 7
Discussion of Week One
The Desire for Discipleship: Why Do We *Want* to Follow Jesus?

Small Group Discussion

Connect

1. Do you know someone whose desire to follow Jesus runs especially deep? If so, what do you think that person has learned that you would like to learn as well?

Confer

2. What in this week's readings did you find especially compelling? Why?

3. So why do *you* follow Jesus?

4. What have you found strengthens your desire to follow Jesus?

   What, if anything, weakens this desire?

Confide

5. How fervent is your desire to follow Jesus these days?

What do you think God is saying to you about this?

Family Discussion

Parents: feel free to adapt these questions to the age and learning style of your kids.

1. If some guy showed up at our front door claiming to be the only person who could give us eternal life, would you put your faith in him? Why or why not?

   Jesus came claiming to be the only person who could give us eternal life. So why do we put our faith in *him*? (Some Scriptures to consult: John 14:6, Matthew 16:15-17, John 6:67-69, Acts 4:12, Philippians 3:8.)

2. What do you know about Jesus that makes you want to follow him?

The Demands of Discipleship:
What Does It *Take* to Follow Jesus?

It does not take much of a man to be a disciple,
but it takes all of him that there is.[1]
DWIGHT PENTECOST

God's grace, his undeserved favor toward us, is the sole basis of our salvation. On this point Scripture is clear. We can't earn our salvation—not even on our best behavior. We can't even contribute to our salvation. Not in the least. Nor is salvation a reward for anything we've done. We have done nothing to deserve it. Nor can we. Salvation is a free gift that can only be received by faith in Christ (Ephesians 2:8-9).

However, that does not mean that Jesus makes no demands of his followers. He does, as we're going to discover in this week's readings. Jesus certainly expects us to obey what he has commanded. But we don't obey *in order to earn* his grace. We obey *in response to* his grace. He always gives us his grace *before* he demands our obedience.[2] In fact, we're not even *capable* of obeying him *until* he gives us his grace.[3]

This week, as we consider the demands of discipleship, let's bear in mind that it's our loving Savior-King who makes these demands of us. He has rescued us and brought us into an intimate and eternal relationship with him. So let's embrace his commands with joy! Let's view them as our delight, because by obeying them we draw near to him.

---

[1]Dwight J. Pentecost, *Design for Discipleship* (Grand Rapids, MI: Zondervan Publishing, 1971), 39.

[2]For a thorough biblical treatment of this subject, see Jonathan Lunde, *Following Jesus, the Servant King: A Biblical Theology of Covenantal Discipleship* (Grand Rapids, MI: Zondervan), 2010.

[3]We'll have more to say about this on Day 24.

Day 8
You Must Be Born Again

I tell you the truth, no one can see the kingdom of God
unless he is born again.
JESUS CHRIST

With these words, Jesus identified the prerequisite for participation in his program: we must be re-born. Until that happens we cannot experience the kingdom of God. But how can a person be "born again"? A religious leader named Nicodemus asked that very question. Clearly, this prerequisite for discipleship is not something we can achieve ourselves. No one can make themselves be born again any more than they could make themselves be born the first time. Clearly, this is something God has to accomplish by his grace.[1]

But it must be received by faith, as Jesus goes on to explain to Nicodemus. In what has become one of the most quoted verses in the Bible, Jesus said, "God so loved the world that he gave his one and only Son, that whoever believes in him shall not perish but have eternal life" (John 3:16).

What does Jesus mean by this? He means that we need to recognize Jesus as God's own Son, the Lord of heaven and earth, sent here to rescue us. And without this Savior, we will perish.[2] And yet Christ's coming also reveals how much God loves us, how desperately he wants to rescue us if we will simply turn to him in faith.

Of course, this turning *to* Jesus in faith implies turning *from* something else. That something else is sin. The *turning from* part is called repentance, and it's the flip side of faith.

I recently set out to find a sandwich shop in an unfamiliar part of town. I had my trusty GPS with me, so I should have had no problem finding it . . . except that I chose not

---

[1] See, for example, 1 Peter 1:3, 23.

[2] In fact, just a few verses later, we read, "Whoever believes in the Son has eternal life, but whoever rejects the Son will not see life, for God's wrath remains on him" (John 3:36).

to use the GPS. I figured I could find it on my own. (You know where this is going, don't you?)

Yes, I got lost. When I finally admitted it and consulted my GPS for help, it had four words for me: *Turn around when possible.*

Not *bear left*. Not *slight right*.

Turn around when possible.

I was going the wrong way, and there was no way to get where I needed to go as long as I continued in the direction I was going.

Turn around when possible. That's what it means to repent and believe in Christ. It means we admit we've gone our own way—the *wrong* way—and we choose to head in a new direction—*his* direction. This was Jesus' message: "Repent, for the kingdom of heaven is near" (Matthew 4:17). The gracious rule and reign of God has drawn near with the arrival of the King himself. It's time to renounce former allegiances and to declare our allegiance to this King once and for all.

This "conversion" is how we know we are born again. And unless we are born again, we cannot see the kingdom of God. Following Jesus begins here.

Reflect

1. Have you been "born again"? How do you know?

2. If you have been born again, take a moment to reflect on the events that led to your conversion, and thank God for how he brought you to faith in Christ.

Remember (our Scripture memory passage of the week)
"Any of you who does not give up everything he has cannot be my disciple" (Luke 14:33).

Day 9
A Whole New Kind of Righteousness

I tell you that unless your righteousness surpasses
that of the Pharisees and the teachers of the law,
you will certainly not enter the kingdom of heaven.

JESUS CHRIST

If you were to ask Jesus' contemporaries, "Who are the models of righteousness?" many would have pointed to the Pharisees and the teachers of the law. After all, they were the professionals at keeping the religious laws. Nobody took their religion more seriously than these guys. So when Jesus said the righteousness of these religious leaders was not good enough, he shocked some people. They must have thought, "If those guys don't meet God's standard of righteousness, then what chance do *I* have of meeting it!"

And yet Jesus' statement, when read in its larger context, sounds more like an invitation than an indictment. It's an invitation to a life of radical righteousness—one that far exceeds anything the religious leaders had ever dreamt of.

Sure, the Pharisees and teachers of the law were the epitome of man-made righteousness. The problem is that man-made righteousness is bankrupt. Jesus doesn't even recognize it as righteousness. In his famous Sermon on the Mount (Matthew 5-7), Jesus forces us to completely reevaluate what it means to be righteous before God. There Jesus says things like, "You have heard that it was said, 'Do not commit adultery.' But I tell you that anyone who looks at a woman lustfully has already committed adultery with her in his heart" (Matthew 5:27-28). He went on to say, "You have heard that it was said, 'Love your neighbor and hate your enemy.' But I tell you: Love your enemies and pray for those who persecute you" (Matthew 5:43-44).

It turns out that Jesus' standard is far more rigorous than anything the Pharisees and teachers of the law ever thought up. *Jesus' standard makes righteousness a matter of the heart—not a matter of mere outward conformity.* As Dallas Willard has pointed out, "Biblical religion is above all a religion of the heart and of the keeping of the heart."[1]

Even if this idea of inward righteousness sounded strange to some, it was not new. In Matthew 5:17, Jesus introduced his statements about true righteousness by saying, "Do not think that I have come to abolish the Law or the Prophets; I have not come to abolish them but to fulfill them." You see, hundreds of years earlier God made a new covenant with his people, in which he promised to write his law on their minds and hearts (see Jeremiah 31:33). Jesus came to make the fulfillment of this covenant possible.

Here again is Christ's grace in action. Through his death and resurrection and the ministry of the indwelling Holy Spirit that followed, Jesus paved the way for a radical inward righteousness. It's a righteousness we can't produce on our own. As the apostle Paul said, "If righteousness could be gained through the law, Christ died for nothing!" (Galatians 2:21).

The right response to Christ's gracious provision of righteousness, then, is to receive this righteousness and to live it out. This is what it takes to follow Jesus.

Reflect

1. How would you describe the kind of righteousness Jesus demands of his followers?

2. How does your soul respond to this truth? Tell God in prayer.

Remember (our Scripture memory passage of the week)
"Any of you who does not give up everything he has cannot be my disciple" (Luke 14:33).

---

[1]Dallas Willard, *The Great Omission*, 108.

Day 10
Giving Up Everything

Any of you who does not give up everything he has
cannot be my disciple.
LUKE 14:33

These are startling words. Give up everything? What does Jesus mean by this? To answer this question, let's consider his statement in its larger context. Here's what he said:

Suppose one of you wants to build a tower. Will he not first sit down and estimate the cost to see if he has enough money to complete it? For if he lays the foundation and is not able to finish it, everyone who sees it will ridicule him, saying, "This fellow began to build and was not able to finish."

Or suppose a king is about to go to war against another king. Will he not first sit down and consider whether he is able with ten thousand men to oppose the one coming against him with twenty thousand? If he is not able, he will send a delegation while the other is still a long way off and will ask for terms of peace. In the same way, any of you who does not give up everything he has cannot be my disciple. (Luke 14:28-33)

Jesus' point is that the decision to follow him must not be entered into lightly. We need to be willing to part with some things. In fact, *all* things will need to be given over to Christ if we are to follow him on his terms. Jesus' point is not that we shouldn't own any material goods but that we should view everything we have—both material and immaterial—as belonging ultimately to Christ. We must hold nothing back from him.

C. S. Lewis put it this way:

Christ says "Give me All. I don't want so much of your time and so much of your money and so much of your work: I want You. I have not come to torment your natural self, but to kill it. . . . I will give you a new self instead. In fact, I will give you Myself: my own will shall become yours."[1]

Dwight Pentecost is right in saying that, "It does not take much of a man to be a disciple, but it takes all of him that there is."[2] The love of Christ demands nothing less.

Were the whole realm of nature mine,
That were a present far too small;
Love so amazing, so Divine,
Demands my soul, my life, my all.
—ISAAC WATTS

Reflect

1. How does the price of discipleship compare to the price of *non*-discipleship?

2. Is there anything you're not willing to give up for Jesus' sake? If so, are you willing to talk to him about it?

Remember (our Scripture memory passage of the week)
"Any of you who does not give up everything he has cannot be my disciple" (Luke 14:33).

---

[1]C. S. Lewis, *The Quotable Lewis*, Wayne Martindale and Jerry Root, ed. (Wheaton, IL: Tyndale House), 571.

[2]Dwight Pentecost, *Design for Discipleship*, 39.

Day 11
Losing Our Life to Find It

Whoever wants to save his life will lose it,
but whoever loses his life for me will find it.
JESUS CHRIST

Among the paradoxes of the Christian life, this one has to be the most perplexing. How is it that striving for something can actually ensure that we never get it? Are you striving to *save* your life? Jesus says forget it. You'll lose it for sure. Are you trying to *lose* your life for Christ? Well guess what. You're not going to lose it. You're going to find it. What sense does that make?

The paradox compels us to look deeper into the meaning of Jesus' statement. There we discover profound wisdom in what he's saying. He's certainly not saying we need to die a martyr's death in order to enter the life he has for us. Physical death is not the point here. He's talking about the key to *life. True* life. And it's not what we expect. It's certainly not what our culture expects. Our culture says, "Find yourself" or "Be true to yourself" or "Take care of yourself." Jesus says if you really want to experience life then *die* to yourself. Give your life over to me. Let me be in charge of your future. As long as you're busy trying to make something of your life you'll miss out on the life I intend for you.

It turns out that clinging to our hopes of realizing our fullest potential is actually the best way to smother those hopes. And the way to really live it up is to be sold out to Christ.

Charles Spurgeon illustrates,

I have seen boys bathing in a river in the morning. One of them has just dipped his toes in the water, and he cries out, as he shivers, "Oh, it's so cold!" Another has gone in up to his ankles, and he also declares that it is fearfully chilly. But see! Another runs to the bank, and takes a header. He rises all in a glow. All his blood is circulating, and he cries "Delicious! What a beautiful morning! I am all in a glow. The

43

water is splendid!" That is the boy for enjoying a bath! You Christian people who are paddling about in the shallows of religion, and just dipping your toes into it—you stand shivering in the cold air of the world which you are afraid to leave. Oh, that you would plunge into the river of life! How it would brace you! What tone it would give you! In for it, young man! In for it! Be a Christian out and out. Serve the Lord with your whole being. Give yourself wholly to him who bought you with his blood.[1]

Reflect

1. Have you seen this paradox played out in some practical way in your life or in someone else's life? If so, how?

2. In practical terms, what might it look like for you to "die to self" and live for Christ?

Remember (our Scripture memory passage of the week)
"Any of you who does not give up everything he has cannot be my disciple" (Luke 14:33).

---

[1]Charles Spurgeon, *Christ's Relation to His People* (London: Passmore & Alabaster, 1902), 144.

Day 12
Holding to His Teaching

If you hold to my teaching, you are really my disciples.
JESUS CHRIST

What's the difference between *talking* about being a disciple and actually *being* a disciple? According to Jesus, the difference is choosing to obey what he says. Discipleship is obedience. G. Campbell Morgan put it this way:

> Advancement is dependent always on our obedience in these hours of testing, in our manifesting in actual practice the power of the truth we have heard in theory. No lesson is considered learned in the school of Jesus which is only committed to memory. That lesson only is learned which is incarnate in the life, and becomes beautiful in its realization and declaration in that way; and until this is so there can be no progress.[1]

So what comes to mind when you hear the word *obedience*? Does it make you think of being forced to do something you don't want to do by someone who has power over you—like the time you tried to get out of eating your vegetables and your mom told you to do it anyway "because I said so"?

You may be surprised to learn that with Jesus obedience is a love word. Obedience is how Jesus expressed his love for the Heavenly Father. He said, "The world must learn that I love the Father and that I do exactly what my Father has commanded me" (John 14:31).

Likewise, obedience is how we can express *our* love for the Father. Scripture says, "This is love for God: to obey his commands" (1 John 5:3). And obedience is also how we show our love for Christ. "If anyone loves me," Jesus said, "he will obey my teaching" (John 14:23).

---

[1]G. Campbell Morgan, *Discipleship* (New York: Fleming H. Revell, 1897), 37.

But obedience isn't easy, is it?

Jesus knows all about it. For him, obeying the Father meant allowing himself to be crucified for our sins. On the night before his crucifixion, being painfully aware of the demands of obedience, Jesus prayed, "Abba, Father, everything is possible for you. Take this cup from me. Yet not what I will, but what you will" (Mark 14:36).

That's what obedience looks like in its purest form. No conditions. No excuses. Just a firm resolve to do what Jesus wants, no matter what—not just because it's our duty but because we love him and because he knows best. When we do that we know we're not just *talking* about discipleship. We're actually *living* it!

Reflect

1. Why do you think obeying Jesus is so important?

2. What has Jesus been teaching you lately that you need to obey him in today?

Remember (our Scripture memory passage of the week)

"Any of you who does not give up everything he has cannot be my disciple" (Luke 14:33).

Day 13
They Will Persecute You Also

No servant is greater than his master.
If they persecuted me, they will persecute you also.
JESUS CHRIST

"Sticks and stones may break my bones, but words will never hurt me." We've all heard that one, haven't we? It usually comes up when we're trying to minimize some verbal attack.

Truth is, for two thousand years Christ followers have been subject to harsh words, beatings, stoning, and worse just because of their faith. Actually, it was no different for Old Testament saints. Scripture says that,

> [Some] were tortured and refused to be released, so that they might gain a better resurrection. Some faced jeers and flogging, while still others were chained and put in prison. They were stoned; they were sawed in two; they were put to death by the sword. They went about in sheepskins and goatskins, destitute, persecuted and mistreated—the world was not worthy of them. They wandered in deserts and mountains, and in caves and holes in the ground. (Hebrews 11:35-38)

Things have not changed that much. While the laws of our nation may provide some protection against religious persecution, many of our Christian brothers and sisters around the world are suffering severe persecution even now. Jesus taught us not to be surprised by this. "If they persecuted me," he said, "they will persecute you also." Some of us will experience more persecution than others, but persecution of Christ followers is here to stay until Christ returns. It goes with the territory.

Whether it comes in the form of verbal ridicule, rejection, or physical violence, Jesus taught us how to deal with the inevitable persecution that will come to us because of our attachment to him. He said,

Blessed are you when people insult you, persecute you and falsely say all kinds of evil against you because of me. Rejoice and be glad, because great is your reward in heaven, for in the same way they persecuted the prophets who were before you. (Matthew 5:11)

Did Jesus really mean we're *blessed* when we're persecuted for our faith in him? And that bit about *rejoicing* and being *glad* when we're persecuted, was he serious about that? [1]

Yes and yes. Whenever you're ridiculed or insulted for Christ's sake you're in very good company. Some of the greatest heroes of the Bible were persecuted too. And when you're persecuted for Christ's sake you can be assured of a hero's reward in heaven.

If you and I are to follow Jesus, we need to be willing to suffer for him. May we never shrink back from persecution for Jesus' sake. He will turn it into a blessing!

Reflect

1. Are you afraid of being persecuted in some way for your faith in Christ? Why or why not?

2. Take a moment to ask Christ for courage to live for him even when it means enduring persecution. Pray also for your brothers and sisters around the world who are enduring severe persecution.

Remember (our Scripture memory passage of the week)
"Any of you who does not give up everything he has cannot be my disciple" (Luke 14:33).

---

[1] See also Philippians 1:29 and 1 Peter 4:16.

Day 14
Discussion of Week Two
The Demands of Discipleship: What Does It *Take* to Follow Jesus?

Small Group Discussion

Connect

1. Growing up, what were some of the reasons you were given for obeying your parents? Were those reasons convincing? Why or why not?

Confer

2. Why should we obey Jesus?

3. How would you describe saving faith in Jesus?

4. Read Luke 14:25-33. Three times in this passage (vv. 26, 27, and 33) Jesus identifies the kind of person who *cannot* be his disciple. Why do you think Jesus spoke this way?

5. What, if anything, in this week's readings did you find especially challenging or controversial? Why?

6. We know that salvation is by grace through faith alone. But what does it take to follow Jesus day by day, in your own words?

Confide

7. What, if anything, hinders your whole-hearted affirmation of Christ as Leader of your life?

Family Discussion

Parents: feel free to adapt these questions to the age and learning style of your kids.

1. All of us have to obey certain rules designed for our own good. Kids have to obey classroom rules at school. Moms and dads have to obey traffic rules while driving. We even have family rules, don't we? Who can tell me one or two of our family rules?

Jesus also has certain "rules" for those who follow him. Who can tell me one or two of Jesus' rules for following him? (Some Scriptures to consult: Matthew 5:20, Luke 14:33, Matthew 16:25, John 14:15.)

2. When do you most want to obey the rules? Is it when the person making the rules is mean and rude? Or is it when the person making the rules cares about you and is trying to help you? Can you think of an example?

3. What kind of person do you think Jesus is? Is he mean and rude or caring and helpful? How do you know?

4. In your heart, do you want to obey Jesus? Why or why not?

5. What is one way you could obey Jesus today?

The Design of Discipleship:
How Does Following Jesus *Work*?

To follow [Christ] is to be learning of him, to think his thoughts, to use his judgments,
to see things as he sees them, to feel things as he feels them,
to be of the same heart, soul, and mind, as he is—
that we also may be of the same mind with his Father . . .
Nothing less is to be his disciple.[1]

GEORGE MACDONALD

I still remember the first (and last) time I tried to change the brakes on my car. "How hard can it be?" I thought. So, I jacked up my Chevy Chevette and tore into it. Several hours later the auto parts store clerk and I were on a first-name basis, my barked knuckles were the same color as my brake lights, and I was overheating like an old clunker by the side of the road.

Somehow, by willpower and brute force, I managed to reassemble the sad thing, new brake pads and all. I was rather proud of myself until the brakes failed the next day. Humbling myself, I took the car to a mechanic who informed me that I had broken a brake piston, leaking brake fluid all over my new brake pads. The whole job had to be redone!

My mechanical blunder was costly and embarrassing. But I did learn a valuable lesson: don't try to fix something if you don't even know how it works. As a result, I've decided to leave all but the simplest automotive repairs to the professionals. It's my way of making our roads a little safer. (I don't blame you for breathing a sign of relief).

I may not know much about automotive repair, but I do know this much: I can't afford to approach my spiritual life as haphazardly as I approached that brake job. But I

---

[1]George MacDonald, *Knowing the Heart of God* (Minneapolis, MN: Bethany House, 1990), 125-126.

can't delegate my spiritual development to a "professional" either. I need to learn how discipleship works if I expect to make any progress.

And so do you.

Let's talk about that this week.

Day 15
Living a New Life

I am the resurrection and the life.
JESUS CHRIST

Jesus did not come to *improve* our life. He came to *give* us life. And there's a big difference between the two. If Jesus came simply to improve our life, we might expect him to build on what we were already doing. Instead, he taught us that there really is no life at all without him. "I am . . . the life" (John 14:6), he told Thomas. And to his friend Martha, Jesus said, "I am the resurrection and the life" (John 11:25), a claim he then proved by raising Martha's brother Lazarus from the dead!

As the "author of life" (Acts 3:15), Jesus often spoke with delight about his mission to impart life to all who came to him. "I have come that they may have life, and have it to the full" (John 10:10), he said. And again, "I give them eternal life and they shall never perish; no one can snatch them out of my hand" (John 10:28).

The "eternal life" that Christ gives us is not simply an *extended* life. It's a fundamentally *different* life. Having received this new life, the apostle Paul says, "I have been crucified with Christ and I no longer live, but Christ lives in me. The life I live in the body, I live by faith in the Son of God, who loved me and gave himself for me" (Galatians 2:20). Paul elaborates elsewhere, saying,

> Don't you know that all of us who were baptized into Christ Jesus were baptized into his death? We were therefore buried with him through baptism into death in order that, just as Christ was raised from the dead through the glory of the Father, we too may live a new life.
>
> If we have been united with him like this in his death, we will certainly also be united with him in his resurrection. For we know that our old self was crucified with him so that the body of sin might be done away with, that we should no longer be slaves to sin—because anyone who has died has been freed from sin. . . .

In the same way, count yourselves dead to sin but alive to God in Christ Jesus. Therefore do not let sin reign in your mortal body so that you obey its evil desires. Do not offer the parts of your body to sin, as instruments of wickedness, but rather offer yourselves to God, as those who have been brought from death to life; and offer the parts of your body to him as instruments of righteousness. (Romans 6:3-7, 11-13)

Here we have the basis—the foundation—for our discipleship to Jesus: we have been given a brand new life to live. This is better than a "do-over." We are not simply given another chance. We now share in Christ's own divine life. It's a life that enables us to live beyond our own selfish, sinful nature, a life that brings us into vital union with Jesus Christ. The apostle Paul summed it up when he said, "If anyone is in Christ, he is a new creation; the old has gone, the new has come!" (2 Corinthians 5:17). As disciples of Jesus, we've been given a new life, a new identity, which is the source of all effective discipleship to Jesus.

Reflect

1. What practical difference does it make that Christ has given you a brand new life?

2. Take a moment to thank God from your heart for the new life he's given you.

Remember (our Scripture memory passage of the week)
"I am the vine; you are the branches. If a man remains in me and I in him, he will bear much fruit; apart from me you can do nothing" (John 15:5).

Day 16
Connecting with God

This, then, is how you should pray:
"Our Father in heaven, hallowed be your name, your kingdom come, your will be done on earth as
it is in heaven. Give us today our daily bread. Forgive us our debts, as we also have forgiven our
debtors. And lead us not into temptation, but deliver us from the evil one."
JESUS CHRIST

Jesus often got alone with the Father to pray (see Luke 5:16), sometimes even spending a whole night in prayer (see Luke 6:12). One day, after observing Jesus pray, his disciples said to him, "Lord, teach us to pray" (Luke 11:1). Jesus responded by giving them a model prayer like the one we find in Matthew 6:9-13.

Notice the prayer begins by addressing God as "our Father in heaven." This is a term of endearment that reminds us that the One to whom we pray is no impersonal force or aloof deity. He is our Heavenly Father, and he welcomes us as his children. So, as R. A. Torrey suggests,

> The first thing to be sure of when we pray is that we really have come into the presence of God, and are really speaking to Him. We should never utter one syllable of prayer, either in public or in private, until we are definitely conscious that we have come into the presence of God and are actually praying to Him.[1]

Having entered the presence of the Father, our first concern is that his name be hallowed—that is, that he be shown the reverence due him. Then we are to align our will with his, praying that he would accomplish what he wants done. Only then does the model prayer turn to asking the Father for his daily provision. The connection between our relationships with others and our relationship with our Heavenly Father is

---

[1] R. A. Torrey, *The Power of Prayer and the Prayer of Power* (Grand Rapids, MI: Zondervan, 1971), 61.

highlighted by the next phrase, which asks him to forgive us according to the measure of forgiveness we extend to others. The model prayer concludes with a plea for God's protection from the temptations and corruptions of this world.

Much more could be said about this model prayer. But even a brief overview reveals that prayer is not about performing a *ritual*. It's about cultivating a *relationship*.

William Law was right:

> Prayer is the nearest approach to God and the highest enjoyment of Him that we are capable of in this life. It is the noblest exercise of the soul, the most exalted use of our best faculties, and the highest imitation of the blessed inhabitants of heaven. When our hearts are full of God, sending up holy desires to the throne of grace, we are then in our highest state, we are upon the utmost heights of human greatness; we are not before kings and princes, but in the presence and audience of the Lord of all the world, and can be no higher till death is swallowed up in glory.[2]

Reflect

1. Which of these aspects of the model prayer gets the most attention in your prayer life? Which aspect is most likely to be neglected? Why is that?

2. What is God saying to you through your reflections on Jesus' model prayer?

Remember (our Scripture memory passage of the week)
"I am the vine; you are the branches. If a man remains in me and I in him, he will bear much fruit; apart from me you can do nothing" (John 15:5).

---

[2]William Law, *A Serious Call to a Devout and Holy Life* (New York: Macmillan and Co., 1898), 144.

Day 17
Seeking First His Kingdom

Seek first his kingdom and his righteousness,
and all these things will be given to you as well.
JESUS CHRIST

If kingdoms reflect the character of their king, then the kingdom belonging to the "King of glory"[1] must be absolutely glorious! And if he is the "King of Kings and Lord of Lords,"[2] then imagine how the majesty of *his* kingdom must eclipse all others! It's no wonder, then, that Jesus would speak of this kingdom as having such surpassing worth that those who find it gladly trade everything they have to be included in it (see Matthew 13:44-46).

In fact, the kingdom of God was the dominant theme of Jesus' preaching.[3] From the time of John the Baptist's imprisonment, Jesus began to preach "Repent, for the kingdom of heaven is near" (Matthew 4:17). And Jesus was still talking about the kingdom right up until his ascension to heaven (see Acts 1:3).

One of the characteristics of the kingdom of God that Jesus taught is that it's not yet fully realized here on earth. His kingly rule and reign is not yet complete in this world. It's in progress, like a tiny mustard seed that grows into a huge plant (see Matthew 13:31-32), like yeast that eventually works its way though the whole lump of dough (see Matthew 13:33).

In the meantime, Jesus calls us to join him in bringing in his kingdom by praying to that end: "Your kingdom come, your will be done on earth as it is in heaven" (Matthew 6:10).

My fellow disciples, one day our Lord will be universally revered as King. His plans will certainly be carried out here, just as they are in heaven. On that day, "Every knee will

---

[1]Five times in Psalm 24 our Lord is referenced by this title.

[2]This is the title assigned to Christ in Revelation 19:16.

[3]The term "kingdom of God" occurs 32 times in the gospel of Luke alone.

bow, in heaven and on earth and under the earth, and every tongue confess that Jesus Christ is Lord, to the glory of God the Father" (Philippians 2:10-11). We pray for the coming of this kingdom. And we seek this kingdom above all earthly pursuits. *This* is our priority, our first and best work.

> *Let goods and kindred go,*
> *This mortal life also;*
> *The body they may kill:*
> *God's truth abideth still,*
> *His kingdom is forever.*
> —MARTIN LUTHER

Reflect

1. In practical terms, what would it look like for you to seek Christ's kingdom and his righteousness above your material pursuits today?

2. Take a moment to ask God to help you do this.

Remember (our Scripture memory passage of the week)
"I am the vine; you are the branches. If a man remains in me and I in him, he will bear much fruit; apart from me you can do nothing" (John 15:5).

Day 18
Humbling Ourselves

Whoever exalts himself will be humbled,
and whoever humbles himself will be exalted.
JESUS CHRIST

Humility, simply defined, is freedom from selfish pride. It's the opposite of self-importance. As William Law describes it,

> Humility does not consist in having a worse opinion of ourselves than we deserve, or in abasing ourselves lower than we really are. But as all virtue is founded in truth, so humility is founded in a true and just sense of our weakness, misery, and sin. He that rightly feels and lives in this sense of his condition lives in humility.[1]

Jesus teaches us that we can humble *ourselves* (and be exalted by him) or we can be humbled *by him* (as a result of exalting ourselves). Either way, learning humility is part of the core curriculum in the school of discipleship to Jesus. Without humility, we will never reflect the character of our Master, who left us the supreme example of humility by submitting to the cross (see Philippians 2:3-11).

But true humility can be elusive, can't it? As soon as you profess to have it, you prove that you don't. Again, William Law says,

> You can have no greater sign of a more confirmed pride than when you think you are humble enough. He that thinks he loves God enough shows himself to be an entire stranger to that holy passion; so he that thinks he has humility enough shows that he is not so much as a beginner in the practice of true humility."[2]

---

[1]William Law, *A Serious Call to a Devout and Holy Life,* 183.
[2]Ibid., 190.

In the end, humility is not at all about self-improvement. It's about self-forgetfulness. It's not about self-entitlement. It's about self-emptying.

John the Baptist captured the essence of humility when he declared, "He [Jesus] must become greater; I must become less" (John 3:30). John teaches me that there is an inverse relationship between *my* glory and *Christ's* glory. The more I glorify myself, the less I can glorify Christ. The less I glorify myself, the more I can glorify Christ. What I *cannot* do is glorify myself and glorify Christ *at the same time*. Many would-be disciples live by the unspoken motto: "Jesus must become greater, and I must become greater too!" This does not work. Discipleship is not a matter of adding Christian goals to my personal agenda. Rather, it's a matter of exchanging my desire to promote self for a desire to promote Christ. The motto of a true disciple is: "he must become more important in my eyes and I must become less important in my own eyes." Only then will others begin to see Jesus in me.

Reflect

1. What would it look like for Christ to increase and you to decrease in your eyes?

2. Take a moment to ask God to bring about these changes in you.

Remember (our Scripture memory passage of the week)
"I am the vine; you are the branches. If a man remains in me and I in him, he will bear much fruit; apart from me you can do nothing" (John 15:5).

Day 19
Abiding in Christ

I am the vine; you are the branches. If a man remains in me and I in him,
he will bear much fruit; apart from me you can do nothing.

JESUS CHRIST

As disciples of Jesus, we are as dependent on him as a branch is dependent on the vine from which it grows. Without him, we can do nothing of any spiritual significance.

To some, this might sound discouraging. But to a genuine Christ follower, it sounds like freedom. Admitting our utter dependence on Christ frees us from our delusion of self-sufficiency. (No one was ever really convinced anyway.) And it clears the way to pursue a wholehearted discipleship to Jesus, one that is not hindered by our foolish pride. Ultimately, the decision to admit our inadequacy and embrace Christ's sufficiency is a decision to leave behind a life that yields nothing of spiritual value for a life that yields much.

That's what remaining in Christ is all about. To *remain*—or as some translations put it, to *abide*—in Christ is to live in utter dependence on him. As R. A. Torrey puts it,

To abide in Christ is to renounce any independent life of our own, to give up trying to think our thoughts, or form our resolutions, or cultivate our feelings, and simply and constantly look to Christ to think His thoughts in us, to form His purposes in us, to feel His emotions and affections in us. It is to renounce all life independent of Christ, and constantly to look to Him for the inflow of His life into us, and the outworking of His life though us.[1]

---

[1]R. A. Torrey, *How to Pray* (Chicago: Moody, 1900), 66.

Living out this radical union with Christ is the key to our spiritual progress. Andrew Murray was a nineteenth century disciple who understood this. Let's listen in on his prayer and make it our own:

> Thou sayest: *Abide in me!* O my Master, my Life, my All, I do abide in Thee. Give Thou me to grow up into all Thy fullness. It is not the effort of faith, seeking to cling to Thee, nor even the rest of faith, trusting Thee to keep me; it is not the obedience of the will, nor the keeping of the commandments; but it is Thyself living in me as in the Father, that alone can satisfy me. It is Thyself, my Lord, no longer before me and above me, but one with me, and abiding in me; it is this I need, it is this I seek. It is this I trust Thee for.[2]

Reflect

1. How does your soul respond to the truth that you can do nothing without Christ?

2. What do you intend to do with this truth? Tell God in prayer.

Remember (our Scripture memory passage of the week)
"I am the vine; you are the branches. If a man remains in me and I in him, he will bear much fruit; apart from me you can do nothing" (John 15:5).

---

[2]Andrew Murray, *With Christ in the School of Prayer* (New York: Fleming H. Revell, n. d.), 166-167.

Day 20
Making Disciples of Others

Go and make disciples of all nations.
JESUS CHRIST

"The world can get on very well without you and me," said D. L. Moody, "but the world can not get on without Christ, and therefore we must testify of Him."[1] The apostles did just that, declaring, "We cannot help speaking about what we have seen and heard" (Acts 4:20).

This, as it turns out, is Jesus' design for *all* his followers. Shortly before Christ's ascension to heaven, he solemnly charged his disciples with these words:

> All authority in heaven and on earth has been given to me. Therefore go and make disciples of all nations, baptizing them in the name of the Father and of the Son and of the Holy Spirit, and teaching them to obey everything I have commanded you. And surely I am with you always, to the very end of the age. (Matthew 28:18-20)

This final charge of Jesus is often called "The Great Commission"—and for good reason. For starters, this commission is great in terms of its *source*: it was issued by the resurrected Lord himself who wields "all authority in heaven and on earth." It's also great in terms of its *scope:* it's a global enterprise, involving "all nations." It's great in terms of its *significance*: it seeks to impart the good news of eternal life through Jesus Christ to people still living in spiritual darkness. The Great Commission is also great in terms of its *surety*: it comes with Christ's personal guarantee that he'll always be with us to ensure our success. But ultimately it's the *supremacy* of the Great Commission that makes it so great: it's not just *a* big deal, it's *the* big deal. It's the Master's master plan for reaching a lost world.

---

[1]Dwight L. Moody, *The Best of Dwight L. Moody*, edited by Ralph Turnbull (Grand Rapids, MI: Baker Book House, 1994), 76.

The point is we can't claim to be following Christ if we're not helping others follow him too. Our calling is both to know Christ and to make him known. We do this by pointing others to faith in Christ and by imparting to fellow believers what *we're* learning in our discipleship to Jesus. Disciples of Jesus make disciples of Jesus. That's why Paul told Timothy, "The things you have heard me say in the presence of many witnesses entrust to reliable men who will also be qualified to teach others" (2 Timothy 2:2).

Charles Spurgeon speaks of the sheer joy of fulfilling this commission:

Even if I were utterly selfish, and had no care for anything but my own happiness, I would choose, if I might, under God, to be a soul-winner, for never did I know perfect, overflowing, unutterable happiness of the purest and most ennobling order till I first heard of one who had sought and found a Savior through my means. I recollect the thrill of joy which went through me! No young mother ever rejoiced so much over her first-born child, no warrior was so exultant over a hard-won victory. Oh! the joy of knowing that a sinner once at enmity has been reconciled to God by the Holy Spirit, through the words spoken by our feeble lips.[2]

Reflect

1. What motivates you to talk to others about Christ?

2. Take a moment to ask God how he might want you to help disciple someone today in some small way. Are you willing to be used in this way?

Remember (our Scripture memory passage of the week)
"I am the vine; you are the branches. If a man remains in me and I in him, he will bear much fruit; apart from me you can do nothing" (John 15:5).

---

[2]Charles H. Spurgeon, *The Soul Winner* (New York: Fleming H. Revell, 1895) 231.

Day 21
Discussion of Week Three
The Design of Discipleship: How Does Following Jesus *Work*?

Small Group Discussion

Connect

1. Share with the group a story about when you tried something but failed because you didn't understand how it was supposed to work.

2. What approaches to discipleship have you pursued in the past? How well have these approaches worked for you?

Confer

3. What misconceptions about discipleship have you encountered along the way?

4. What, if anything, in this week's readings did you find especially helpful? Please explain.

Confide

5. What do you think are the greatest hindrances to your progress in discipleship?

6. When do you feel especially close to Jesus?

7. As you reflected on this week's readings, did God reveal to you some aspect of your discipleship to Jesus that you need to approach differently? If so, what is he showing you?

Family Discussion

Parents: feel free to adapt these questions to the age and learning style of your kids.

1. Think about your best friendships. What has made those friendships work so well?

2. What do you think it takes to have a close friendship with Jesus? (Some Scriptures to consult: Matthew 6:1, Matthew 6:33, Matthew 23:12, John 15:5, Matthew 28:19.)

3. What do you think is the hardest part about following Jesus? Why?

4. If Jesus were here in person, what would you ask him to help you with so you could follow him more faithfully? Take a moment to ask him for this in prayer.

The Dynamics of Discipleship:
What *Enables* Us to Follow Jesus?

Train yourself to be godly.
1 TIMOTHY 4:7

Continue to work out your salvation with fear and trembling,
for it is God who works in you to will and to act
according to his good purpose.
PHILIPPIANS 2:12-13

Somewhere between Tonka trucks and 1500-piece puzzles, my dad gave me my first ready-to-assemble plastic model. My young imagination was captivated by the glossy picture on the box top of an army jeep bounding over rough terrain. I was sure I could create a masterpiece every bit as exciting as the one in that picture. All I needed was a little time with the pieces that were in the box.

My dad suggested we work on it together, but I didn't think that was necessary. So, while he was away at work, I settled into his desk chair with model glue and hobby knife in hand, figuring I would complete this work of art by the time Dad got home.

Opening the box, I was surprised to find only a hodgepodge of dull-looking plastic parts. Somehow I thought the pieces would be more recognizable and more polished. I couldn't even tell what most of the pieces were! And for a minute I thought of waiting for my dad's help.

But only for a minute. Then my naïve self-confidence kicked in again and I decided that this was *my* project and that I had better get busy. In my haste, I only glanced at the detailed instructions that were included with the kit. They looked too complicated anyway. I starting cutting and gluing.

Soon into the process, my confidence began to wane and I thought about consulting the instructions.

"Naa." I kept gluing.

I attached the wheels to the chassis but smeared glue all over the tires and the axles. Once they dried, the wheels wouldn't spin like they were supposed to. I sighed and tried to console myself.

Then I glued the windshield. Trying to rub off the excess glue only made it worse. "It doesn't look anything like the jeep in the picture!" I fumed. "I'm gonna smash this thing! How could my dad give me this stupid thing when it's impossible to put together!" Unwilling to admit that it was my fault, I put the model away and pretended the whole thing never happened.

Eventually, I told my dad about the fiasco, and with his help I learned an important lesson that applies to my discipleship to Jesus as well. It's good to have a compelling picture of what I'm working toward. But getting there is going to require some outside help. This week, we're going to identify the resources we need to succeed in our discipleship to Jesus.

Day 22
The Word of God

Sanctify them by the truth; your word is truth.
JESUS' PRAYER FOR HIS DISCIPLES

What would you think of someone who claimed to be a follower of some great spiritual master but was not familiar with that master's teachings? Weird, huh?

It goes without saying that someone identifying himself or herself as a disciple should be at least somewhat (if not thoroughly) familiar with what that master actually teaches. And so it is with us. As disciples of Jesus, it's our business to know well what Jesus taught and to come under that teaching.

So where do we go to learn what Jesus taught? Secular historians have recorded some of this information, but the only "authorized"[1] biographies of Jesus are found in the Scriptures. While the entire Bible points us to Jesus Christ,[2] the Gospels (Matthew, Mark, Luke, and John) record the actual events of Jesus' earthly life and ministry, including his teachings.[3] As part of the Holy Scriptures, the Gospels are inspired by God himself and are designed for our progress in the faith. The apostle Paul tells us that,

> All Scripture is God-breathed and is useful for teaching, rebuking, correcting and training in righteousness, so that the man of God may be thoroughly equipped for every good work. (2 Timothy 3:16-17)

---

[1]By *authorized*, I mean divinely inspired, recorded by an apostle of Christ (or a close associate of an apostle), and recognized as authentic by the early church.

[2]According to Luke 24:27, Jesus himself explained this to a couple of his disciples on the road to Emmaus after his resurrection.

[3]The historical reliability of these Gospels has been well documented. See, for example, Craig L. Blomberg, "The Historical Reliability of the New Testament," in *Reasonable Faith: Christian Truth and Apologetics*, ed. William Lane Craig (Wheaton, IL: Crossway, 1994), 193-231.

So, we read the Scriptures expecting them to thoroughly equip us to follow Jesus. But we also expect the Scriptures to "read" us, because

The word of God is living and active. Sharper than any double-edged sword, it penetrates even to dividing soul and spirit, joints and marrow; it judges the thoughts and attitudes of the heart. (Hebrews 4:12)

We don't need to wonder what Jesus taught. His precepts have been recorded and preserved for us in the Scriptures—particularly in the Gospels. The only question is, *Are we taking the time to really learn them?*

Reflect

1. What role is the Bible supposed to play in the life of a disciple of Jesus?

2. Do you spend enough time listening to God speak to you from the Scriptures? How do you know?

Remember (our Scripture memory passage of the week)
"Since we live by the Spirit, let us keep in step with the Spirit" (Galatians 5:25).

Day 23
The Son of God

I have set you an example that you should do as I have done for you.
JESUS CHRIST

God has not only given us the instructions for discipleship in the Bible. He's also given us a perfect real life example. Jesus' own life is the model for how a disciple should live. As Michael Wilkins says,

> To become a fully human and fully alive person, then, we pattern ourselves after Jesus. He is the complete revelation of the image of God (Colossians 1:15-20), and at the same time He is the one person whose humanity was never spoiled by sinning (Hebrews 4:15). Since the outworking of the image of God is seen most fully in Jesus, we should pattern ourselves after Him.[1]

So, how can we take after Jesus? There are a couple of ways we can imitate our Master.

First, we can imitate Jesus' *progress*. Even though Jesus was the Son of God, the Bible says that he "grew in wisdom and stature, and in favor with God and men" (Luke 2:52). That is, in his humanity, Jesus experienced intellectual growth (he grew in "wisdom"), physical growth (he grew in "stature"), spiritual growth (he grew in "favor with God"), and social growth (he grew in "favor with men").[2] Part of what it means to imitate Jesus' example, then, is to seek to grow in all areas of life.

Second, we can imitate Jesus' *practices*. A careful reading of the Gospels reveals that spiritual disciplines were an important part of Jesus' life. What are spiritual disciplines? According to Dallas Willard, "Spiritual disciplines are activities in our power that we

---

[1]Michael J. Wilkins, *In His Image: Reflecting Christ in Everyday Life* (Colorado Springs, CO: NavPress, 1997), 119.

[2]Ibid., 120.

engage in to enable us to do what we cannot do by direct effort."[3] Much like physical exercise enables us to grow stronger and more physically fit, spiritual disciplines enable us to grow more spiritually fit. Luke tells us that, "Jesus often withdrew to lonely places and prayed" (Luke 5:16). Apparently, prayer and solitude were among Jesus' regular spiritual disciplines, as were fasting,[4] fellowship,[5] and serving.[6]

Now if the Son of God felt the need to engage regularly in certain spiritual disciplines, then what does that say about our need of the same? The apostle Paul encouraged Timothy to take this seriously, saying, "Train yourself to be godly. For physical training is of some value, but godliness has value for all things, holding promise for both the present life and the life to come (1 Timothy 4:7-8).

Reflect

1. How eager are you to grow in all areas of your life? Are there areas you're neglecting?

2. Is there a particular spiritual discipline that you'd like to practice to help you grow stronger spiritually? If so, what is it and how do you plan to put this into action?

Remember (our Scripture memory passage of the week)
"Since we live by the Spirit, let us keep in step with the Spirit" (Galatians 5:25).

---

[3]Dallas Willard, *The Great Omission*, 52.

[4]See, for example, Matthew 4:2.

[5]Jesus lived his life in close fellowship with his disciples, as evidenced throughout the Gospels. See also Luke 4:16.

[6]See, for example John 13:15.

Day 24
The Grace of God

My grace is sufficient for you,
for my power is made perfect in weakness.
JESUS CHRIST

As important as spiritual disciplines are to our spiritual growth, you and I can't *cause* our spiritual growth any more than a farmer can *cause* his crops to grow. The best a farmer can do is to understand and submit to the natural laws God has established. The farmer can cultivate the soil, plant good seed, tend the plants, and harvest the crops when it's time. If he's a good farmer, he will do these things diligently and in the proper order. Still, he can't *make* the plants grow. In fact, he can't even fully explain how it happens.

The same is true of our spiritual growth. Though we eagerly do those things that are known to foster spiritual growth, we can't *make* growth happen. At most, the practice of spiritual disciplines opens us more fully to Christ's work in our lives. And ultimately it's *his* work that produces the spiritual growth we desire. The apostle Paul reminds us that it was God who began a good work in us and it is he who will carry it on to completion until the day of Christ Jesus (Philippians 1:6).

The Bible has a word for this mysterious, growth-inducing power of God at work in us. That word is *grace*. When the apostle Paul was at the end of his rope, Christ told him, "My grace is sufficient for you" (2 Corinthians 12:9). It always is.

God's grace is his unmerited favor, and it manifests itself toward us in many different ways. Yes, his grace is the basis of our forgiveness. But it's more than that. His grace is behind every blessing we'll ever receive. In fact, his grace is behind every positive step we'll ever take on our journey with Christ. So Peter says, "grow in the grace and knowledge of our Lord and Savior Jesus Christ" (2 Peter 3:18). Without Christ's grace there can be no spiritual progress.

Charles Spurgeon says,

Every good thing that is in a Christian not merely begins but progresses and is consummated by the fostering grace of God, through Jesus Christ. If my finger were on the golden latch of paradise, and my foot were on its jasper threshold, I should not take the last step so as to enter heaven unless the grace which brought me so far should enable me fully and fairly to complete my pilgrimage.[1]

This grace of Christ at work in us is his way of enabling our progress as his disciples. So, Paul exhorts us to "continue to work out your salvation with fear and trembling, for it is God who works in you to will and to act according to his good purpose" (Philippians 2:12-13).

Reflect

1. In what ways do you see God's grace enabling you to grow as a disciple of Jesus?

2. Are there areas of your life in which you might be resisting God's sufficient grace, relying instead on your own strength? If so, take a moment to ask God to open your heart to his sufficient grace in those areas.

Remember (our Scripture memory passage of the week)
"Since we live by the Spirit, let us keep in step with the Spirit" (Galatians 5:25).

---

[1]Charles H. Spurgeon, *The Metropolitan Tabernacle Pulpit: Sermons Preached and Revised by C. H. Spurgeon*, vol. 15 (London: Passmore & Alabaster, 1908), 291.

Day 25
The Spirit of God

You will receive power when the Holy Spirit comes on you.
JESUS CHRIST

Sometimes I envy those original disciples who got to be with Jesus, to hear him speak, to see his facial expressions, to observe what made him laugh and what made him weep. Oh, how I wish I could have been there! If only he were here now, in person! What could possibly be better than that?

Actually, there is something even better than that. Jesus told his disciples, "It is *for your good* that I am going away. Unless I go away, the Counselor [the Holy Spirit] will not come to you; but if I go, I will send him to you" (John 16:7, italics added). And in a post-resurrection appearance, Jesus told his disciples to go nowhere until they were baptized with this promised Holy Spirit (Acts 1:3-5). He then told them why: "*You will receive power when the Holy Spirit comes on you*; and you will be my witnesses . . ."[1] (verse 8, italics added). Clearly, the Holy Spirit's power is the key factor in this "go, no-go" scenario.

As promised, the Holy Spirit showed up a few days later, as recorded in Acts 2, and the disciples were enabled to do things they were incapable of doing on their own. Perhaps the most astounding example of the Spirit's transforming effect is seen in Peter. Here's a guy who, a few days earlier, had disowned Jesus (see Matthew 26:69-75) and ended up cowering in fear in a locked room with the other disciples after Christ's crucifixion (see John 20:19). But now that Peter is filled with the Spirit, he boldly preaches the gospel to a large crowd, which resulted in about 3,000 people becoming Christ followers (Acts 2:14-41)! That's the difference the Holy Spirit makes.

Since then, the baptism of the Holy Spirit has become the normal experience of all Christ followers. The apostle Paul wrote, "We were all baptized by one Spirit into one

---

[1]This, of course, is exactly what happened, as the rest of the book of Acts goes on to record.

body—whether Jews or Greeks, slave or free—and we were all given the one Spirit to drink" (1 Corinthians 12:13).

While the Bible never commands Christians to be *baptized* with the Holy Spirit (because we already are), it does command us to be *filled* with the Spirit. Paul says, "Do not get drunk on wine, which leads to debauchery. Instead, be filled with the Spirit" (Ephesians 5:18).[2]

But what does this mean? Notice that being filled with the Spirit is contrasted with being drunk with alcohol. When a person is drunk (that is, full of alcohol), the alcohol has control over that person, as reflected in the way he or she talks and behaves. Likewise, when a person is filled with the Spirit, that person is controlled by the Spirit. Being filled with the Spirit, then, is not about "filling our tanks" with more of the Spirit. We already have all of the Holy Spirit. Rather, it's about giving the Holy Spirit more of *us*. It's about "being under the influence"—not the influence of alcohol but the influence of the Spirit.[3]

Jesus knew that we would need the Holy Spirit to carry out his work in this world, so he gave us something better than his physical presence. He gave us the Holy Spirit.

Reflect

1. How aware are you of the Holy Spirit's influence in your life?

2. Think of an area of your life (maybe a relationship or a habit) that you want to see transformed. Take a moment to ask God to fill you with the Holy Spirit and to bring about the transformation you seek.

Remember (our Scripture memory passage of the week)
"Since we live by the Spirit, let us keep in step with the Spirit" (Galatians 5:25).

---

[2]See also Galatians 5:16.

[3]Examples of Christians being filled with the Holy Spirit include Peter (Acts 4:8), Stephen (Acts 6:5), Barnabas (Acts 11:24), Paul (Acts 13:9), and the disciples (Acts 13:52).

Day 26
The Family of God

Whoever does the will of my Father in heaven is
my brother and sister and mother.
JESUS CHRIST

To become a disciple of Jesus is to become part of a new family, the family of God (see 1 John 3:1). In fact, Jesus spoke of the bond between members of this "faith family" as surpassing even those of our biological family:

> While Jesus was still talking to the crowd, his mother and brothers stood outside, wanting to speak to him. Someone told him, "Your mother and brothers are standing outside, wanting to speak to you."
>
> He replied to him, "Who is my mother, and who are my brothers?" Pointing to his disciples, he said, "Here are my mother and my brothers. For whoever does the will of my Father in heaven is my brother and sister and mother." (Matthew 12:46-50)

What an amazing truth, that Jesus would call us his true brothers and sisters!

This, of course, means we are brothers and sisters to one another as well. The New Testament writers took this to heart. They not only referred to their fellow believers using family terms.[1] They also had plenty to say about how we should treat our brothers and sisters in Christ. Relational phrases like "one another" and "each other" show up dozens of times in the New Testament. For example, the writer of Hebrews says, "Encourage one another daily, as long as it is called Today, so that none of you may be hardened by sin's deceitfulness" (Hebrews 3:13). How easy it is to lose our perspective when we neglect our relationships with our fellow disciples!

---

[1]The apostle Paul, for example, referred to fellow believers as "brother" (see 1 Corinthians 15:58, Colossians 1:1, and Colossians 4:9), "sister" (see Philemon 2 and Romans 16:1), "son" (see Philemon 10, Philippians 2:22, and 2 Timothy 1:2), and "mother" (see Romans 16:13).

But the most pivotal "one another" of all is found in John 13:35, where Jesus says, "By this all men will know that you are my disciples, if you love one another." The implication is that disciples who decide to "go it alone" are not only jeopardizing their chances of staying the course as a disciple. They are already off mission. A loner disciple is a contradiction in terms. We need each other if we're going to follow Jesus. God designed it that way. Joseph Hellerman spells it out:

> Spiritual formation occurs primarily in the context of community. People who remain connected with their brothers and sisters in the local church almost invariably grow in self-understanding, and they mature in their ability to relate in healthy ways to God and to their fellow human beings. This is especially the case for those courageous Christians who stick it out through the often messy process of interpersonal discord and conflict resolution. Long-term interpersonal relationships are the crucible of genuine progress in the Christian life. People who stay also grow.[2]

It turns out that doing life together in community is not only a *good* idea. It's *God's* idea. We need each other if we're going to thrive in our discipleship to Jesus.

Reflect

1. How Christian fellowship strengthened your discipleship to Jesus?

2. Are you giving fellowship with other believers the priority it deserves in your life? What is God saying to you about this?

Remember (our Scripture memory passage of the week)
"Since we live by the Spirit, let us keep in step with the Spirit" (Galatians 5:25).

_____

[2]Joseph Hellerman, *When the Church Was a Family* (Nashville, TN: B & H Publishing, 2009), 1.

Day 27
The Armor of God

My prayer is not that you take them out of the world
but that you protect them from the evil one.
JESUS' PRAYER FOR HIS DISCIPLES

Jesus made it clear that we have a spiritual enemy, calling him "the evil one." Elsewhere the Bible refers to him as "the devil" or "Satan." Jesus taught us to pray for protection from this enemy (see Matthew 6:13), which he modeled by praying for the spiritual protection of his disciples (see John 17:15).

God is certainly able to protect us from our enemy, as the apostle Paul assured the Thessalonian believers, "The Lord is faithful, and he will strengthen and protect you from the evil one" (2 Thessalonians 3:3). But in Ephesians 6:10-18, Paul identifies how we must put this spiritual protection into practice. Take a moment to read and reflect on what he says in this passage.

> Finally, be strong in the Lord and in his mighty power. Put on the full armor of God so that you can take your stand against the devil's schemes. For our struggle is not against flesh and blood, but against the rulers, against the authorities, against the powers of this dark world and against the spiritual forces of evil in the heavenly realms. Therefore put on the full armor of God, so that when the day of evil comes, you may be able to stand your ground, and after you have done everything, to stand. Stand firm then, with the belt of truth buckled around your waist, with the breastplate of righteousness in place, and with your feet fitted with the readiness that comes from the gospel of peace. In addition to all this, take up the shield of faith, with which you can extinguish all the flaming arrows of the evil one. Take the helmet of salvation and the sword of the Spirit, which is the word of God. And pray in the Spirit on all occasions with all kinds of prayers and requests. With this in mind, be alert and always keep on praying for all the saints. (Ephesians 6:10-18)

This, then, is how we stand our ground and experience the spiritual victory Christ has won for us. We must take up the spiritual armor Christ provides. This includes truthfulness, righteousness, peace, faith, salvation, and the Scriptures. Against such things the evil one cannot prevail. As Charles Spurgeon warns,

> You may be of a very quiet spirit, but your adversaries are not so. If you attempt to play at Christian warfare, they will not. To meet the powers of darkness is no sham battle. They mean mischief. Nothing but your eternal damnation will satisfy the fiendish hearts of Satan and his crew. You must take not so much a flag to unfurl, or a drum to beat, as a sword to use, and a specially sharp sword too. In this combat, you will have to use a sword such as even evil spirits can feel, capable of dividing asunder of soul and spirit, and of the joints and marrow.[1]

Let us, then, take up this armor. And let us fight the good fight of faith, knowing that victory is ours in Christ Jesus!

Reflect

1. According to Paul, why do we need to put on the full armor of God? What's the point of doing so?

2. Does one of these pieces of spiritual armor strike you as being especially important to you right now? If so, why?

Remember (our Scripture memory passage of the week)
"Since we live by the Spirit, let us keep in step with the Spirit" (Galatians 5:25).

---

[1]Charles H. Spurgeon, *The Metropolitan Tabernacle Pulpit*, vol. 37, 235.

Day 28
Discussion of Week Four
The Dynamics of Discipleship: What *Enables* Us to Follow Jesus?

Small Group Discussion

Connect

1. Can you think of a time when you tried to build or fix something without the right tools? How did it go?

Confer

2. Practically speaking, how can each of the enabling dynamics discussed in this week's readings make a difference in our discipleship to Jesus?

   The Word of God

   The Son of God

   The Grace of God

The Spirit of God

The Family of God

The Armor of God

3. Which of these enabling dynamics do you think is most likely to be neglected?

Confide

4. What in this week's readings struck you as being especially significant to your discipleship to Jesus right now? Why?

5. Going forward, how do you intend to make good use of the resources God has provided for your discipleship? What, if any, practical steps could you take to accomplish this?

Family Discussion

Parents: feel free to adapt these questions to the age and learning style of your kids.

1. Can anyone think of a time when you tried hard to do something but you just couldn't do it? What happened? What would have helped you to be able to do it?

2. What would it be like to have to dig a well with a spoon or to build a house with a screwdriver? (frustrating!)

   It's important to have the right tools for the job, isn't it? The same is true when trying to follow Jesus. What has Jesus given us to help us follow him? (Some Scriptures to consult: 2 Timothy 3:16-17, John 13:15, 2 Corinthians 12:9, Acts 1:8, Hebrews 10:25, Ephesians 6:10-18.)

3. How could we make better use of the help God gives us to follow Jesus?

The Destiny of Discipleship:
What *Happens* When We Follow Jesus?

Many live as enemies of the cross of Christ. Their destiny is destruction . . .
But our citizenship is in heaven. And we eagerly await a Savior from there, the Lord Jesus Christ,
who, by the power that enables him to bring everything under his control,
will transform our lowly bodies so that they will be like his glorious body.
THE APOSTLE PAUL

There's a song in my heart that my lips cannot sing,
  'Tis praise in the highest to Jesus my King;
Its music each moment is thrilling my soul,
  For I was a sinner, but Christ made me whole.

I shall stand one day faultless and pure by His throne,
  Transformed from my image, conformed to His own;
Then I shall find words for the song of my soul,
  For I was a sinner, but Christ made me whole.

A sinner made whole! A sinner made whole!
  The Savior has bought me and ransomed my soul!
My heart now is singing; there's joy in my soul,
  For I was a sinner, but Christ made me whole.
—WILLIAM M. LIGHTHALL

Day 29
Becoming Like Jesus

A student is not above his teacher,
but everyone who is fully trained will be like his teacher.
JESUS CHRIST

So what exactly is Jesus, our Teacher and Master, trying to do with us, his disciples? He gives us a clue when he says that, "Everyone who is fully trained will be like his teacher" (Luke 6:40). The purpose of discipleship is to make us more like Jesus—or, as the apostle Paul put it, for Christ to be "formed" in us (Galatians 4:19).

George MacDonald elaborates,

To follow [Christ] is to be learning of him, to think his thoughts, to use his judgments, to see things as he sees them, to feel things as he feels them, to be of the same heart, soul, and mind, as he is—that we also may be of the same mind with his Father. . . . Nothing less is to be his disciple.[1]

Imagine thinking the way Jesus thinks, speaking the way he speaks, relating the way he relates, doing what he does. What a transformation that would be!

The apostle Paul often referred not just to the *possibility* but the ongoing *necessity* of this transformation.[2] Clearly, this is the point of our discipleship to Jesus. In light of this, Dallas Willard offers this advice:

Examination of our ultimate desires and intentions, reflected in the specific responses and choices that make up our lives, can show whether there are things we hold more important than being like him. If there are, then we are not yet his disciples.[3]

---

[1]George MacDonald, *Knowing the Heart of God*, 125-126.

[2]See especially Romans 8:29, Romans 12:22, and 2 Corinthians 3:18.

[3]Dallas Willard, *The Spirit of the Disciplines* (San Francisco: Harper Collins Publishers, 1988), 265.

Brothers and sisters, our transformation is already underway! And it must continue until Christ takes us home to heaven. Only then will the transformation be complete. "What we will be," says the apostle John, "has not yet been made known. But we know that when he appears, *we shall be like him*, for we shall see him as he is" (1 John 3:2, italics added).

> *Oh to be like Thee! Oh to be like Thee!*
> *Blessed Redeemer, pure as Thou art;*
> *Come in Thy sweetness, come in Thy fullness;*
> *Stamp Thine own image deep on my heart.*
> —THOMAS O. CHISHOLM

Reflect

1. What, if anything, about becoming like Jesus stirs your soul?

2. What's one area of your life in which you're hoping to experience some transformation? Take a moment to share this with Christ in prayer.

Remember (our Scripture memory passage of the week)
"A student is not above his teacher, but everyone who is fully trained will be like his teacher" (Luke 6:40).

Day 30
Inexpressible and Glorious Joy

Though you have not seen him, you love him;
and even though you do not see him now, you believe in him and are filled with an inexpressible
and glorious joy, for you are receiving the goal of your faith, the salvation of your souls.
THE APOSTLE PETER

Following Jesus is not a quest for happiness. Happiness is fleeting anyway. When we follow Jesus, we discover something better. We discover joy.[1] Inexpressible and glorious joy. We experience this joy despite hardships.[2] We even experience this joy *because* of hardships,[3] knowing that these difficulties are designed to make us "mature and complete" (James 1:4).

Jesus never said the life of a disciple would be easy. But he *did* say that it would be marked by joy, that it would be a *blessed* life. Jesus made this clear in his first recorded sermon (see Matthew 5-7). We know it as "The Sermon on the Mount." The very first word of that sermon is the word "blessed." In fact, Jesus used that word nine times in the opening section of the sermon[4] to refer to those who manifest the values of the kingdom of heaven. There Jesus paints a portrait of who we are becoming as his disciples. It's a picture of the kind of person God approves, the kind of person on whom his favor rests. From the start, Jesus calls us to a life that's blessed in ways this world knows nothing about. In fact, we've been blessed with "every spiritual blessing in Christ" (see Ephesians 1:3).

But ultimately, the anchor and source of our joy is not the blessings Christ gives us. It is Christ himself. *He* is our joy.

A. W. Tozer is right:

---

[1] Passages that speak of this joy include Matthew 13:44, Luke 2:10, Luke 10:17, Luke 24:52, John 15:11, John 17:13, Acts 16:34, 2 Corinthians 8:2, and Philippians 1:25-26.

[2] See, for example, 1 Peter 1:6.

[3] See especially Matthew 5:11-12, Romans 5:3-5, 2 Corinthians 12:10, James 1:2-4, and 1 Peter 4:13.

[4] This section, Matthew 5:3-12, is often referred to as "The Beatitudes."

The man who has God for his treasure has all things in One. Many ordinary treasures may be denied him, or if he is allowed to have them, the enjoyment of them will be so tempered that they will never be necessary to his happiness. Or if he must see them go, one after one, he will scarcely feel a sense of loss, for having the Source of all things he has in One all satisfaction, all pleasure, all delight. Whatever he may lose, he has actually lost nothing, for he now has it all in One, and he has it purely, legitimately and forever."[5]

The closer we draw to Christ, the closer we draw to the source of our joy. This, my fellow disciples, is our destiny.

Reflect

1. How does your soul respond to the truth that following Christ leads to joy?

2. Could you be missing out on joy because you're looking for it in the wrong places? Take a moment to ask God to reveal to you whether this may be true and what to do about it.

Remember (our Scripture memory passage of the week)
"A student is not above his teacher, but everyone who is fully trained will be like his teacher" (Luke 6:40).

---

[5]A. W. Tozer, *The Pursuit of God* (Harrisburg, PA: Christian Publications, 1948), 20.

Day 31
Building Our House on Bedrock

Everyone who hears these words of mine and puts them into practice
is like a wise man who built his house on the rock.
JESUS CHRIST

Life is dangerous and unpredictable. The sheer magnitude of the insurance industry is a testimony to our fear of some unforeseen catastrophe befalling us. We have life insurance, health insurance, disability insurance, homeowners insurance, and auto insurance, just to name a few.

But there's another kind of insurance that's more foundational than all of these. And it's free. Call it "endurance insurance," if you like. Jesus spoke about it at the end of his Sermon on the Mount. He said,

> Therefore everyone who hears these words of mine and puts them into practice is like a wise man who built his house on the rock. The rain came down, the streams rose, and the winds blew and beat against that house; yet it did not fall, because it had its foundation on the rock. But everyone who hears these words of mine and does not put them into practice is like a foolish man who built his house on sand. The rain came down, the streams rose, and the winds blew and beat against that house, and it fell with a great crash. (Matthew 7:24-27)

Notice that Jesus' illustration assumes that there will be storms. The question is not whether our foundation will be tested. It will. The question is whether our foundation will hold, whether we will endure. Jesus recognizes only two approaches to life. One leads to destruction. The other leads to security and stability.

The life of security and stability belongs to those who hear Jesus' words and put them into practice. The disciple of Jesus builds his life on the bedrock of Christ's teachings. As the old hymn puts it,

On Christ the solid rock I stand,
    All other ground is sinking sand.
All other ground is sinking sand.
  —EDWARD MOTE

Reflect

1. How does your soul respond to the truth that obeying Jesus' teachings leads to true stability and security?

2. What is God saying to you through Jesus' illustration of the wise man and the foolish man?

Remember (our Scripture memory passage of the week)
"A student is not above his teacher, but everyone who is fully trained will be like his teacher" (Luke 6:40).

Day 32
Bearing Good Fruit

This is to my Father's glory, that you bear much fruit,
showing yourselves to by my disciples.
JESUS CHRIST

"We don't smoke. We don't chew. And we don't go with girls who do." That about sums up what some people think it means to be a Christian. In their minds, what sets a Christ follower apart is what he or she does *not* do.

I don't know about you, but this doesn't ring true in my experience. I know plenty of people who don't smoke or chew who aren't Christ followers. I also know some Christ followers who smoke and chew.

Jesus said we show ourselves to be his disciples by bearing much fruit. But we can get so focused on keeping the weeds out of the vineyard that we forget to check to see if there's even any good fruit growing there. As one writer put it, "True spirituality does not consist in what one does not do, it is rather what one does. It is not suppression: it is expression. It is not holding in self: it is living out Christ."[1]

"Make a tree good and its fruit will be good," Jesus said, "or make a tree bad and its fruit will be bad, for a tree is recognized by its fruit" (Matthew 12:33). The point is that a true disciple of Christ can be recognized by the good fruit of his or her life—fruit that's consistent with the character of Christ.

The apostle Paul refers to this good fruit as "the fruit of the Spirit." He says, "The fruit of the Spirit is love, joy, peace, patience, kindness, goodness, faithfulness, gentleness and self-control" (Galatians 5:22-23). These virtues, which the Holy Spirit produces in us, are the fruit of our discipleship to Jesus.

And as we saw on Day 19, our fruitfulness is inevitable when we remain in Christ. Jesus promised that "If a man remains in me and I in him, he will bear much fruit" (John

---

[1]Lewis Sperry Chafer, *He That is Spiritual* (Wheaton, IL: Van Kampen Press, 1918), 68.

15:5). As Andrew Murray points out, "If Christ, the heavenly Vine, has taken the believer as a branch, then He has pledged Himself, in the very nature of things, to supply the sap and spirit and nourishment to make it bring forth fruit."[2]

A true disciple *will* bear good fruit. We have Christ's word on it.

Reflect

1. What, if any, connection have you observed between the quality of your discipleship to Jesus and the spiritual fruitfulness of your life?

2. Where is the fruit of the Spirit most evident in your life right now? Where is it least evident? What is Jesus saying to you in light of this?

Remember (our Scripture memory passage of the week)
"A student is not above his teacher, but everyone who is fully trained will be like his teacher" (Luke 6:40).

---

[2]Andrew Murray, *Abide in Christ* (Fort Washington, PA: Christian Literature Crusade, n. d.), 115.

Day 33
A Heavenly Reward

Behold, I am coming soon! My reward is with me,
and I will give to everyone according to what he has done.
JESUS CHRIST

A great many people spend their lives striving for earthly carrots—carrots like affluence, prestige, comfort, security—only to realize in their twilight years that the carrot was rotten. Even more tragic is that many will *never* come to this realization—at least not in this life.

King Solomon put his finger on the problem. "God has set eternity in the hearts of men" (Ecclesiastes 3:11), Solomon said. Nothing temporal can truly satisfy us—not money, not the praise of men, not any earthly trophy. We yearn for something eternal, transcendent.

Jesus promises his followers just such a reward for their faithfulness in serving him in this life.[1] His reward is not of this world. It's heavenly, incorruptible, eternal, and it answers perfectly and completely the "eternity" God has set in our hearts.

Actually, Scripture speaks of our heavenly reward in a couple of different ways. On the one hand, the apostle Peter spoke of "an inheritance that can never perish, spoil, or fade—kept in heaven for you" (1 Peter 1:4). The apostle Paul tells us that the Holy Spirit dwelling in us serves as a deposit guaranteeing our inheritance (Ephesians 1:13-14). In other words, our heavenly inheritance could not be more secure!

On the other hand, the apostle Paul spoke of a heavenly "prize" worth striving for. He said, "Forgetting what is behind and straining toward what is ahead, I press on toward the goal to win the prize for which God has called me heavenward in Christ Jesus" (Philippians 3:13-14). Like Paul, none of us has reached perfection. We're still in process.

---

[1]Jesus promises this reward in Revelation 22:12. The apostle Paul identifies the occasion of this reckoning as "the judgment seat of Christ" (2 Corinthians 5:10).

So we strive toward the goal of our discipleship, like an athlete running to win, knowing that our Lord will reward us some day.

We don't know when that day will be, but Jesus calls us to keep watch.[2] It could be today!

Reflect

1. How does your soul respond to the biblical promise of your heavenly reward?

2. If you knew Jesus was coming back today, what, if anything, would you do differently? Take a moment to speak to God about this in prayer.

Remember (our Scripture memory passage of the week)

"A student is not above his teacher, but everyone who is fully trained will be like his teacher" (Luke 6:40).

---

[2]See, for example, Matthew 16:27 and Matthew 24:42.

Day 34
A Heavenly Reunion

In my Father's house are many rooms; if it were not so, I would have told you.
I am going there to prepare a place for you. And if I go and prepare a place for you,
I will come back and take you to be with me that you also may be where I am.

JESUS CHRIST

Home. That's where we're going. There Jesus is preparing a special place for us in the Father's house. There we will join the jubilant multitude of the redeemed from every age. There we will meet Jesus face to face. There we will spend eternity with our Savior. What a reunion that will be!

To the Christ follower nothing could be more thrilling than the prospect of being welcomed into our heavenly home by Christ himself. But this is more than a hopeful prospect. It's as certain as anything we know. On Christ's promise, we *will* reach our destination. Until then, we press on in hopeful expectation, because "Here we do not have an enduring city, but we are looking for the city that is to come" (Hebrews 13:14). Or, as the apostle Paul it, "Our citizenship is in heaven. And we eagerly await a Savior from there, the Lord Jesus Christ" (Philippians 3:20).

E. M. Bounds says,

To the true Christian, heaven is not a mere sentiment, or poetry, or dreamland, but real solid and abiding granite in strength, home-drawing in sweetness and influence. . . . What does God think of us who have no sighings for heaven, no longings for it; earth, earthly, earthened? God's throne is in heaven. His power, person and glory are preeminently there. Does God attract and hold us? Then heaven attracts and holds. Do we thirst after God?[1]

---

[1]E. M. Bounds, *Heaven: A Place—A City—A Home* (NY: Fleming H. Revell, 1921), 108-109.

John Donne once wrote, "No man ever saw God and lived; and yet, I shall not live till I see God; and when I have seen him I shall never die."[2] This is the hope and destiny of every disciple of Jesus. Praise be to God!

> *Soon will our Savior from Heaven appear,*
> > *Sweet is the hope and its power to cheer;*
> *All will be changed by a glimpse of His face;*
> > *This is the goal at the end of our race.*
> —ADA R. HABERSHON

Reflect

1. How does your soul respond to this truth that Christ is preparing a place in heaven for you?

2. Take a moment to thank God for this hope you have in him.

Remember (our Scripture memory passage of the week)
"A student is not above his teacher, but everyone who is fully trained will be like his teacher" (Luke 6:40).

---

[2]John Donne, *Donne's Sermons: Selected Passages With an Essay by Logan Pearsall Smith* (Oxford: Clarendon Press, 1919), 224.

Day 35
Discussion of Week Five & Wrap-up
The Destiny of Discipleship: What *Happens* When We Follow Jesus?

Small Group Discussion

Connect

    1. What's one thing you're looking forward to right now?

Confer

    2. Did this week's readings give you something to look forward to? If so, what is that?

    3. Which, if any, of the outcomes of following Jesus that we read about this week did you find especially compelling? Why?

    4. What, if anything, in this week's readings do you think merits further study?

Confide

5. If following Jesus means becoming like him (Luke 6:40), then what aspect of Jesus' character are you most eager to emulate?

6. What in this week's readings struck you as being especially significant to your discipleship to Jesus right now? Why?

7. How has this Orientation to Discipleship Campaign strengthened your discipleship to Jesus? What insights or encouragement have you gained? What new attitudes or habits are you forming as a result of the experience?

Family Discussion

Parents: feel free to adapt these questions to the age and learning style of your kids.

1. Who do you want to be like when you grow up?

Do you want to be like Jesus? Why or why not?

2. What does the Bible say will happen to us if we follow Jesus? (Some Scriptures to consult: Luke 6:40, 1 Peter 1:8, Matthew 7:24, John 15:5, Revelation 22:12, John 14:2-3.)

3. Which of the outcomes of following Jesus do you most look forward to? Why?

Afterword

*By finding Christ we have found the route to our final destination, but
there is much traveling yet ahead. We are both finders and seekers,
having found our Lord only to begin our search in earnest.*[1]

R. C. SPROUL

Congratulations on completing this Orientation to Discipleship! Together, we've taken a significant step in our discipleship to Jesus. But this is just the beginning. Remember, this is only an *orientation*. Discipleship is, after all, a lifelong pursuit.[2] There's so much more to learn, so much more Jesus wants to teach us!

To help you take next steps in your discipleship to Jesus, the Intentional Discipleship Series will soon release a comprehensive set of small group studies like this one. Collectively, these "guided expeditions" are designed to teach us to obey everything[3] Jesus commanded (Matthew 28:19-20).

So stay tuned!

And may our Lord bless you as you continue following him!

For more information, contact Dave Steel at:
imstainlesssteel@gmail.com
www.davesteelblog.com

---

[1] R. C. Sproul, *The Soul's Quest for God* (Wheaton, IL: Tyndale House Publishers, 1992), 203-204.

[2] At the conclusion of his earthly ministry, Jesus was still exhorting Peter, "Follow me!" (John 21:19, 22).

[3] By *everything*, we don't mean "exhaustively" but we do mean "comprehensively," as in "every major topic Jesus addressed."